DEAR DESTINY

Letters of Strategy and Tools
for Building Your Best Self

Sha'Malia Willis
Foreword by Dr. Cindy Trimm

It's a lot of work to be a teenager and young adult. Although it's just a short time of your life's journey on earth, these years set the tone for which path you will take. Let's journey together and get you on the best path.

TABLE OF CONTENTS

FOREWORD

Dear Destiny is the first installment of a series of books designed to help young girls navigate life. Growing up in poverty, I know the power of a book to elevate one's life. Books were my lifeline. They opened up new worlds of possibility that enabled me to dream big. Everything I achieved, became and acquired was the result of pulling wisdom and principles from the personalities and characters I read about. Those books provided me with a unique type of literary mentorship. In reading *Dear Destiny*, I immediately thought how important ShaMalia Willis' work will be to the many girls sure to benefit from this form of mentorship. If I had had such a book—one that distilled and clearly articulated foundational success principles—I would have quantum leaped my progress, and perhaps avoided unnecessary hiccups along the way.

Refreshingly authentic and incredibly relatable, this book will deeply influence any reader interested in defying the expectations of what it means to be a young woman today. *Dear Destiny* holds up a mirror to many aspects of teen life and "adulting." Written as a collection of letters, each weekly narrative connects with specific themes and problems from the perspective of an adult personality whose experiences and vantage points provide the framework for rich, heart-to-heart conversations. The scenarios are thoughtfully curated perspectives that provide a platform for deepening conversations and guiding classroom discussions. The practical, easy-to-apply advice is like hearing from a friend when dealing with some of the toughest issues teen girls may face—from body image to unexpected pregnancy.

Dear Destiny is an intimate, thoughtful guidebook that speaks to anyone struggling with bullying, peer pressure, siblings, parents, friends, school, dating and decision-making. The accompanying journal gives readers an avenue to open up and express their vulnerability in a way that empowers them to successfully navigate their thoughts and feelings. In the author's words, "These letters serve as a guide to accessing the keys needed to see the bigger picture so you can make wise decisions for a more promising future. You can push a little further, go a little harder, and make a difference when you see the bigger picture." *Dear Destiny* offers pearls of wisdom that delightfully challenge young readers to think about the world and how to live in it successfully.

On a personal note, beyond loving this book and highly recommending it as a must-read by every teenage girl, I also recommend that parents, educators, pastors and priests read it and gift it to every young girl you influence. I highly recommend this book because it is authored by someone who is not only a brilliant teacher, but actually lives what she teaches brilliantly. What makes this book a must-read is that its author, Ms. ShaMalia Willis, is the personification of every lesson, every instruction, every principle offered within its pages.

– N. Cindy Trimm
Bestselling Author, Humanitarian & Consultant

THANK YOU

"The words, *Thank You*, to another is a pleasant wind of appreciation, and a kiss of gratitude; there are no other words necessary."

Thank you to my mother and father, who only accepted the best from me. You both are the oil and water that created the balance of my temperament, which birthed the woman I am today. I love you both.

To my family, we are all a perfect blend.

To my siblings, Donna, Jamea, KeAndrea, James Jr., and Paris, you all are always ready to go along for the ride. Oh, Paris, who would listen to my stories, support my pop-up businesses and try my prototypes without question. You left us too soon. I love you and thank you for believing in me.

To Bishop Elect Marvin L. Winans, I "won" with you in my life since adolescence. You taught me to never be ashamed of truth and to live a life uncompromising.

To my future children and future husband, I was thinking of you in advance. I work hard to be a fine, upstanding mother and wife you all can be proud of. I pray that one day, you can rise and call me "blessed."

To my beautiful goddaughters, Zaya Monet Trimm, Tae'Lah Cawthon, and Lateka Robinson, I look forward to our trips around the world.

To my "Golden Girls," Karen Gay, Mary Nizio and Brenda Stith, who only viewed me as "perfect" until I caught on. You all

3

loved me beyond my flaws and taught me to love myself without interruption. Everything was a lesson learned.

To the educators who took great care of me during my adolescent years: Lina Cammon, Dr. Dedria Willis, Elaine Wilmore, Deborah Perry, Catrina Walker, Carolyn Lipscomb, Charlotte Smith, Tanya Moss, Charlotte Harfoot, Dr. Karen McEwen, Dr. Mark Sperling, Jen Newell and Delores Leapheart, Esq. The Bible states that "my people are destroyed for lack of knowledge" (Hosea 4:6). Well, you all have given me so much life. Thank you!

To every teacher who educated me, encouraged me, disciplined me, and loved me, I'm forever grateful. I teach with each of your styles combined.

To every friend who added light to my torch so I could continue this journey, thank you. To my amigas, to my God-given sisters and brothers, you all are my true daily cheerleaders.

To the amazing Rho Mu Chapter of Delta Sigma Theta Sorority, Inc., and the great Detroit Alumnae Chapter thank you for giving me a platform to serve.

To the trailblazers who pointed toward the mark for me: Em Walker, Melinda Gooch, Dr. Dorie McKnight (for striking the match), Dr. Ty Adams, Toy Banks, Jillian Blackwell, Glenda Curry, Gwenda Sheard, Dr. Medina Pullings, Dr. Francine Pender, Dr. Lorie Johnson and Ms. Clarice Huckstep, oh, Ms. Clarice.

To every young person I've had and have the pleasure to serve by teaching, you sharpen my wit and keep me "hip," but most of all, you make life worth living.

To Principal Kearney, thank you for pushing me to the finish line. I'm most grateful.

To my "work sister," NaKeisha Woods-Green, and to all my colleagues and staff, you're valuable and make life so much better.

To Dr. Cindy Trimm, I'm in awe of God's love for me, that He graced me with the honor of having you in my life. You've been consistent; you've taught me to own my truth and opened my eyes to the unimaginable. Thank you for inviting me to every single continent and loving me beyond words. What an amazing godmother and mentor you are to me!

"Never love anyone who treats you like you're ordinary."

– Oscar Wilde

Dedicated to Mrs. Karen Yvonne Gay
(who passed the torch to me):
You went the distance with me and believed in me. The words
manifested because you imprinted them in a beautiful book in
1996 and they nestled within my soul.
I'm eternally grateful to have you in my life.

Sha'Malia Willis

Dedicated to my beautiful niece, Tamia Lewis.
I pass the torch to you and your generation.
You're the greatest part of my *destiny*. Your journey inspired me
to write this book and empower every young adult to dream,
wake up and live big.

Tamia, receive wisdom and search out truth; that's where you
will find your uniqueness. Honor those who have gone before
you. Make yourself and the almighty God proud; the rest of the
world will catch up.

DEAR DESTINY

I went to Australia not only to finish writing the letters, but to take a moment with God and ensure that I'm leading you on a path that will intersect with your destiny. I want to show you how you can do this thing called life the right way. I walked in His footsteps, so I want to share what He allowed me to experience.

Dear Destiny,

Welcome to the world of unlimited possibilities! I am excited to share that from the beginning, you were given everything you needed to succeed in this thing called *life*! When you were a baby, you were given your Father's DNA, and He is rich! You possess an inexhaustible treasure that guarantees everything you do will work together for your good!

Today, you may face that fear of riding an elevator past the 10th floor or speaking before 35,000 people. It's time to push past limits and exceed expectations; but most importantly, exceed *your own* expectations. You have what it takes to stand up and show out. Leadership is not reserved for a particular race, gender or culture—but for the one who dares to grasp the assignment and make it their own. I can't imagine the countless number of individuals who will follow once you begin to lead.

We can't choose who brings us into this world, and we may not learn from the individuals we desire to teach us, but wisdom will yield itself to us when we're ready. Every young lady should be equipped with strategies for living, facing fears, making friends, taking care of their body, having non-negotiables, exploring the world and living out loud in truth and boldness.

Each day is an opportunity and, today, you can be courageous. This journey can mark that moment when your life changed for the better. You will become the leader who commands your audience to be accountable for their actions. You will gain a new sense of love, freedom, discipline, bravery and fearlessness. You will lead by example and will encourage a life of etiquette for generations to come.

I have been writing letters for years, waiting for the right opportunity to put them all in a book to help young women who need words of encouragement and wisdom. *Dear Destiny* details some of my personal experiences, along with those of my mentors. Although I can share some lessons with you, the best lessons are the ones you'll experience yourself. Just like in school, it's up to you to pass your tests.

These letters serve as a guide to accessing the keys needed to see the bigger picture so you can make wise decisions for a more promising future. You can push a little further, go a little harder, and make a difference when you see the bigger picture. The key unlocks potential and helps you to choose truth over convenience. Challenge the masses and, you, my dear, can have it all. I want to grant you access and allow you to stand on the backs of the "trailblazers" to see the land of opportunity and dreams unimagined. I have the wisdom keys needed to unlock the possibilities.

Once you gain access, you can see a world of unlimited possibilities and make positive decisions that will impact your life.

Together, we will learn the best practices and tools for making the best decisions in any situation. From knowing which fork is yours and the importance of high self-esteem, to how to interview for your first babysitting position and how to code an app, we will dive into all things *"girl power."* Whatever your parents and guardians had to tiptoe around, we understand and will address head on.

I am in Australia right now, pulling on my godly genes to finalize the last of the fifty-two letters, which are *"Letters of Strategy and Tools for Building your Best Self"* I've written one letter for each week to cover as many situations, emotions and seasons you may possibly endure throughout adolescence. Hopefully, the wisdom shared throughout this book will last you a lifetime and, who knows? There may be a "Volume Two" later.

I pray you gain comfort and wisdom from these *Letters of Etiquette for Life.*

LEADERS

To My Dearest Daughter,

From the beginning of life, we are given leaders; a set of parents, a polite neighbor or a kind teacher. No matter the family structure, adopted or not, we all grow up differently and ultimately follow someone else's example.

The key is *understanding*. We must understand that parents and/or guardians can only give us what they've been given and their roles can be so complex. Every leader plays a role, but not all situations are created equally. Some adolescents don't have parents to offer them advice, and others have questions that they dare not ask any adult. If you turn to a friend who lacks in wisdom because they can only see through a "keyhole," they can't take you any further than they've gone because they have a limited view of life and experience.

You must decide to live a life based on honesty and integrity. Because they're written with so many diverse backgrounds, reading these letters will allow you to reach the best conclusions based on your individual life experiences. There are so many paths to choose from. Many have taken paths that caused them to fall victim to their environment, consequently becoming a statistic. There are those who take the path less traveled; they are living disciplined lives, creating a plan, pushing the envelope, bending the rules, and setting a new bar. These are great men and women who dare to lead; they sit at tables and change countries with the stroke of a pen. Choose the path that lines up with your destiny. If you can't find it, carve out your own path.

I thought about every individual who gave me a chance, who trusted me above my age and pay grade, and allowed me to push past limits. My family was, and is, indispensable; they were absolutely necessary in building who I am today. For me, family was the first foundation laid for me. From there, every mentor, teacher, boss, coach and friend made a difference. There were tough days, sleepless nights, deadlines and breakthroughs, and I learned early on that every single situation shaped the woman who I would become. I also learned that everyone needs a wise mentor.

As I sat on the steps of a high peak of the Great Wall of China exhausted but yet so free, I thought, *What were the odds that I would have the opportunity to make my dreams a reality?* Who taught me to dream big, beyond the space I existed in? What was that innate feeling that told me I was destined for greatness? I attribute my success to every amazing mentor who crossed my path either physically, through a book, or afar. Having great mentors in my life has always been humbling and made the difference. My mentors each came at the perfect time in my life, and I trust that you will have the same experience.

I had a middle school teacher by the name of Karen Dobbins Gay. She was a phenomenal teacher who taught music, English, and even an afterschool French group. It's safe to say that I spent a great amount of time in her classroom.

I wasn't the easiest student to have, however. I was talkative and loved to dance around. Although my behavior at times should have landed me right in detention, it never did. Instead, Mrs. Gay would tell me every profession that I would benefit from by using my gift of speech, my height to model and/or my dancing to compete. She had the patience of Job and a strategy that changed countless lives.

At age twelve, none of the options she offered were a priority, but her *words* stuck with me. I didn't know that her releasing those words would give me something to hold on to and create a path to success for me. Ten years later, I stood in front of Mrs. Gay and her colleagues and gave a commencement speech to the graduating class at my alma mater just because someone believed in me and spoke over my path.

This year, I would like to be your mentor. Allow me to walk you through this portion of your journey and get you over the hurdles you may encounter. After you come through victorious, you can do the same for the next person. One day, someone will look to you as a mentor. As you continue to overcome obstacles and inspire people with your story you will motivate others who'll say, "If you can do it, I can do it."

When it comes to my mentors, their passion to pursue their callings fueled me, and their ability to choose their battles taught me. This world is full of teachers; some have endured rigorous semesters of higher academia, and others were students of life. Time and experience for both produced *wisdom*. Think about the path you desire to take and the others that you dare not even consider taking. Imagine how you want your future to look. Every individual who comes into your life is a teacher; learn from all of them.

Learn from the teachers, friends and even those who have chosen to call you an enemy. They each hold a valuable lesson, all adding to the fuel, whether it be diesel, special, supreme, propelling you forward. Remember that where you are now *is not* where you will be once you complete this book. Here's the charge: Before you begin to read another letter, before you go to the next level, ask yourself the following questions and answer them honestly:

Am I loving myself?
Who in my life matters most?
How am I imagining my future?
What lessons are my mentors teaching me? Am I taking notes?
Am I putting the strategies I've been taught to good use?

I am so very blessed to have people in my life who are present. They make themselves available whenever they can, and that means a lot. I want the same for you—a village that will never allow you to be mediocre. Being average is such a disappointment to your full potential. You have the ability to be amazing in your future career path, community and family. "Average" doesn't open doors or allow you to excel, and it doesn't define the woman you will one day become. Daughter, you're destined for cutting-edge greatness.

LETTER 2
ACCESS GRANTED

Dear Destiny,

I remember your dad putting you on his shoulders during those hot summer softball games so you could see what all the cheering was about. When all the kids would rally around the ice cream stand, he would lift you so you could make your selection before it was your turn.

When you were about three, you started choosing other methods to lift yourself to attain the things you were so desperately reaching for or wanting to see. No matter how great your vision was, your stature only allowed you to stand on the tips of your toes and see through a limited amount of space.

During our most recent talk, you shared how you looked through the keyhole of the old library and could see the dusty furniture with a burst of sunshine that had pushed its way through the heavy golden drapes. If I asked you what was in the room, and how the furniture was arranged, you would vividly describe what your eye beheld while you kept the other tightly shut to get a good focus.

My daughter, you had a limited view from your position. There was so much more in that room that you had no idea existed much less could even see. That room contained numerous books that opened my mind to a world to which I could only dream of traveling as a small girl. That room contained the books I read to my grandmother who would smile faintly and fall asleep as she listened. There's much more for you to see in the days to come.

For so long, I desired to be a pilot. I read books, watched videos, saved pictures as my screensaver and posted pictures on my vision board. One day, during a casual vending machine chat, my boss Dr. Darryl Sawyers overheard me speaking of my desire to fly. For my birthday, he gave me the greatest gift ever—a flight with lessons to follow. Shortly after going up and taking a couple of lessons, everything stopped because I received an offer for a full-time position with a company in Atlanta. I talked to my boss and assured him that at some point, I would continue my lessons in warm Georgia or return to Michigan soon to finish what I had started.

After a few years, I completed my assignment on location in Georgia and began to work from home. Shortly after, I began to live in between Georgia and Michigan. While in Michigan, I visited the Tuskegee Airmen National Historical Museum with 45 of my etiquette students. To my surprise, Dr. Brian Smith, the president of the museum, invited my students to attend the Young Eagles program that offered a free ride in an airplane. After a couple trips to the airport, I began to volunteer, chaperoning and offering math tutoring to the youth in aviation.

That same year, I attended the EAA world's largest airshow in Wisconsin. I was wowed! I'm talking about access to the world of aviation. I was standing in the middle of an opportunity of a lifetime. At that moment, I realized that at one time, I was only seeing a limited view of the aviation community; however, because a few individuals allowed me to stand on the shoulders of their hard work and success, I was awarded an opportunity along with a glimpse of my future.

Upon our arrival back home I hurried to sign up for that years upcoming ground school with Mr. Fazal Khan. I later joined the Civil Air Patrol Detroit 100th Composite Squadron. I took it all in, my focus had led what I loved to find me while I was in search of it.

Remember how you kept one eye tightly shut to get a good focus through the keyhole? Sometimes, you must shut out things like negativity, time wasters, social media and peer pressure to sharpen your focus. Focus until the opportunity comes and you're given access.

LETTER 3
YOU

You are responsible for the name attached to your fingerprint.

Dear Destiny,

I once asked my mentor, "What was one of the most important lessons you've learned in life?" She quoted the words of Dr. Maya Angelo: "When someone shows you who they are, believe them the first time."

Stop trying to figure people out once they've proven themselves; however, this was said with a disclaimer. We must always give people room to grow—that's called mercy. Some individuals prove themselves to be loyal, disloyal, helpful, or non-trustworthy. Good, bad and indifferent actions speak much louder than words. Every person is responsible for themselves, so you can't be so overtaken by their choices. You are responsible for your own life.

First things first. *You must be yourself.* I must admit that I used to pick up other individuals' habits so quickly—their quirks, sayings and gestures, among other things. I would have to catch myself and just *stop*. I'd think to myself, "That's not even me." I laugh at myself because I know how things can slowly change you.

One day, it's just a word or two and the next thing you know, you've taken on a person's full persona, hand gestures, smirks, profanity and all. It's so easy to do but you must abstain from doing so. You owe it to yourself to be your authentic self. If it doesn't fit your personality and you're uncomfortable with any new habits, just make a conscious decision to stop repeating the bad habit and adjust.

I found the most strength in taking a moment to detach myself from everyone else and find my identity: *Who am I?* I didn't want to let God down and fail to discover my true purpose and identity.

Let me go back. When I was a young girl, I just knew I would be the next Oprah. However, through life and wisdom, I came to the best conclusion that *Oprah* is the next Oprah. It's not a problem to study a person's strengths and incorporate them into your daily activities, but it's important to not lose yourself. Great morals, being kind and ethical, timely, patient, and forgiving are great habits and manners to adopt. Mixing these positive attributes with your own uniqueness makes a recipe for long-term success. Oprah taught me from afar the true essence of timing, perseverance and being yourself.

You must be yourself; you are the only one who holds your DNA and exact fingerprint. No one can live your life like you can. You were born to be great in your own skin. You can carve out your own path to your destination. The hurdles you will overcome and triumphs you will endure will give you an amazing testimony for others to overcome.

Let's take a moment and identify where you are and where you're headed.

STEP 1
WHO AM I?

Answer the following questions pertaining to a personal S.W.O.T. (Strengths, Weaknesses, Opportunities and Threats) Analysis to the best of your ability.

Strengths: What am I good at? What strengths do I possess?
Example: Creative, reliable people-person, team player

Weaknesses: What am I not so good at? What weaknesses do I possess?
Example: Unpunctual, fear of speaking in front of others, procrastination

Opportunities: What's available to me to assist me in making better decisions? What opportunities do I possess?
Example: Extracurricular activities at school, apps to improve punctuality, job openings that match my skill set.

Threats: What's keeping me from achieving my goals? What's threatening my success?
Example: Low-ranking test scores, suspension due to tardiness

STEP 2

Choose six words that best describe you.

Example: curious, grateful, driven, outspoken, positive, innovative, artsy, intentional, intelligent, loving, smiley, trustworthy, garrulous, joyful, sharp, alive, indecisive

_____	_____
_____	_____
_____	_____

Choose six words that best describe who you are *not*.

Example: unforgiving, disorganized, dramatic, suspicious, insecure, curious, driven, outspoken, positive, innovative, complex, depressive, demanding, lazy, short-tempered

_____	_____
_____	_____
_____	_____

What do you like? Out of the many adjectives you used to describe yourself, also note what you like most about being associated with those adjectives.

Example: What I like most about being kind is that when I show kindness to others, I feel as if that kindness always returned to me.

What do you dislike? You may have chosen a term that was not so flattering, but here's the beautiful thing. You can create an opportunity and change that weakness into a strength.

Example: I would like to work on my patience so I can be better equipped to endure tests and trials.

What is your purpose? Why are you here? What fuels you? In what ways are you creative?

Example: My purpose is to provide a safe place for people to come and share their triumphs so others can be encouraged. I'm a great listener.

You are absolutely a world changer, and the world needs *you—the authentic you!* Let's continue this journey as we try to better ourselves daily, and we will circle back later to view the answers above.

TAKE CARE OF YOURSELF

Dear Destiny,

As I fly around the world, something always remains constant on each flight; the flight attendant grabs the mic and exclaims the following guidelines:

> *"Oxygen and the air pressure are always being monitored. In the event of a decompression, an oxygen mask will automatically appear in front of you. To start the flow of oxygen, pull the mask towards you. Place it firmly over your nose and mouth, secure the elastic band behind your head, and breathe normally. Although the bag does not inflate, oxygen is flowing to the mask. If you are travelling with a child or someone who requires assistance, secure your mask on first, and then assist the other person. Keep your mask on until a uniformed crew member advises you to remove it."*

You can't see that oxygen, but in case of an emergency, it will help you take your next breath. The same faith you have in that oxygen is the same faith you must have in yourself. Take another breath and live! That faith will give you the fuel you'll need to push yourself forward in creating the most amazing vision for your life. You must believe you can do anything you put your mind to. Believe that you will give your best and pass every test life throws at you. There is no time to be defeated. When life kicks you down, do yourself a favor and jump back up. You were created to be a champion and push the limits. You were created to stand up for yourself and stand out from the rest.

On each flight, the aircrew always encourages the passengers to first save themselves. Doing this enables them to save another person's life. This is also true in life. We are all placed in this world to be a help to one another. One thing I've learned is that *people always need help.* The question is: Are you going to position yourself to help others, offer false expectations or burn yourself out?

Before offering help, you must first be in the right position to do so. You must be well-rounded and healthy before trying to help others. You have to first ensure your oxygen mask is on and that you are breathing in order to be beneficial to others.

Before helping someone who is battling depression, you must be mentally healthy. Make sure you have no debt and provide an agreement before loaning money to anyone—especially if you don't have it to lose. Since we are on this topic, let me make it clear: *Never loan anyone anything you are not willing to lose.* Don't let anyone's debt bring *you* into the land of debt. Although you're young, the earlier you become familiar with finance, the better. We will address this more in depth later.

There's nothing wrong with sacrifice within mutually beneficial relationships. If you're hungry and can sacrifice a portion of your meal, then by all means, use discernment and go for it. Remember, if you can't help a person, you can always point them toward another resource that can.

Allow me to share the story about "The Great Samaritan" (Luke 10:30-35, The Message):

Jesus answered by telling a story. "There was once a man traveling from Jerusalem to Jericho. On the way he was attacked by robbers. They took his clothes, beat him up, and went off leaving him half-dead. Luckily, a priest was on his way down the same road, but when he saw him he angled across to the other side. Then a Levite religious man showed up; he also avoided the injured man. "A Samaritan traveling the road came on him. When he saw the man's condition, his heart went out to him. He gave him first aid, disinfecting and bandaging his wounds. Then he lifted him onto his donkey, led him to an inn, and made him comfortable. In the morning he took out two silver coins and gave them to the innkeeper, saying, 'Take good care of him. If it costs any more, put it on my bill—I'll pay you on my way back.'...."

The Good Samaritan was the perfect person to fully assist the injured man. He didn't come by with just a word of encouragement or to drop off a warm meal—both of which are beautiful kind gestures of love and care. He was skilled in first aid. He had the strength to lift him and the finances to help, and even bring back more if necessary. Lending a helping hand is a beautiful opportunity to bless others and opens up the door for someone to do the same for you; however, make sure you're in a good position to assist those around you.

Pray
Spiritual

Read a Book
Intellectual

Ride a Bike
Physical

Positive Thoughts
Emotional

Journal
Social

Listen to Positive
Podcast
Financial

Community
Gardening
Environmental

LETTER 5
YOU FIRST

Dear Destiny,

A person can feel what you feel about yourself. It's in your walk, your talk, and the way you project your voice. Sometimes, it's in your inability to make eye contact when you speak. How you treat yourself determines the boundaries you place on others. What are your expectations? How do you allow people to treat you?

If you love taking care of your hair, you probably choose wisely when it comes to *whom* you allow to style it. When you love yourself, you will automatically choose what you will tolerate or reject. That girl in the mirror deserves to be pampered, respected, given second chances, friendship, mercy, and *love*. While you are putting out love, encouragement and empowerment, understand that you deserve the same encouraging advice you give others. Say it aloud:

I can do it.
Life is waiting on me.
I have what it takes.
I am beautiful and I continue to become more beautiful each day.

Trust Yourself

Adolescence can be somewhat of a difficult journey. At a certain stage, your parents start to let go of your hand so you can learn to walk on your own. You also learn how many things your parents decided for you and actually protected you from. And now, you must make those same great decisions for yourself. Life will teach you lessons that are most important for you to be a successful, well-rounded individual. You will always have those amazing "A-ha!" moments that will open your eyes to the big picture that brings maturity and growth.

Push Yourself

Sometimes, you may have to go at it alone. You may also have to do it scared. Either way, you must push yourself to get the job done. You were born with the gene to become a leader and world changer. Mediocrity is not in your genes. It takes work and sheer grit to find your place.

We have an internal GPS-like system. This system is called "unease." It will continuously alert us if we are off our path. It's necessary to stay on course. You must persevere because your life and livelihood depend upon you facing your fears and reaching your goals. Someone is watching you—not just your trials, but the way you endure and triumph to reach your desired destination. Your story is significant, and your decisions will all be pen to paper one day. Make yourself proud—it's up to you to make your life count.

Approve Yourself

When others know you need approval, they will use that insecurity to manipulate and control you. You can't give people that type of control over your life. It's your job to become captain of your own ship and learn to dominate your own waves. Approve yourself, love yourself, remember yourself and take care of yourself.

Be Great

When you get your annual physical, which doctor would you choose? An average doctor or one who has excelled in his or her schooling and profession? Things change often in the medical field; there are new breakthroughs every day. You don't want an old remedy with bad side effects when a new one is available to heal the underlying ailment and make you whole again. The only way your doctor will have knowledge of better treatment is if he or she keeps up with their schooling and latest breakthroughs in modern medicine. So, just like you wouldn't choose an average doctor over a great one, you have a responsibility to provide the same greatness for the product or service you will provide one day. Be great and continue to better yourself. You are always a work in progress. Your life is worth the living. So *be great!* You will be chosen out of the crowd and picked over average.

Being Average

Average is not an option!

LETTER 6
WRITE THE VISION

Dear Destiny,

I have you in mind with everything I do. I wonder about what goals you're achieving back home, and I look forward to seeing you soon.

Speaking of writing, remember the vision board parties I used to host annually? I decided to do a digital one here. Have you begun writing out the steps you will take to achieve the things you've placed on your vision board for this year? Although we created short-term vision boards, this is a great time to discuss long-term vision boards as well. We so often think about a vision for ourselves, but your life will impact so many others that this may include writing a vision for your future corporation. You may also have to write a vision for the role you will play in the world in which you live.

I'm looking up at the beautiful stars, thinking about Botswana. Everything about Botswana seems big; someone had a big vision. The land mass is there waiting for someone to write its future business, financial and community systems into existence. What I love most about Botswana is its rich history and that it was destined to be great—just like you.

There are just over two million people in Botswana. It gives the feeling of being a little fish in a big pond. It's not because the population is great. It's the land mass in comparison. Gaborone, the capital, is where the party is going on. It is home to over 10% of that population. Botswana was one of the poorest countries in the world, but fast forward to the discovery of diamonds there, since 1966, Botswana continues to maintain one of the world's highest economic growth rates.

You may be too young to recall, but Her Excellency Tebelelo Mazile Seretse was our guest. She was the ambassador of the Republic of Botswana to the United States, not to mention the first woman appointed into the position. The ambassador had a heart for the youth. She tried to give them the best education that life could afford them. Education is important; it opens doors unimaginable. When you learn, you garner the opportunity to finally see yourself where you desire to be. Hence, the reason I speak so heavily on the importance of you attaining knowledge. Someone has to be bold enough to cast the vision for the home, community, city, state, region, country, continent and the world. Why can't that person be *you*? Place it on your vision board, write the timeline for the plan, and execute.

Former Prime Minister Lee Kuan Yew, who governed Singapore for three consecutive decades, transitioned his nation from a third-world country to first-world country in a single generation. He had the same 24 hours a day that you've been given. He decided to make it count; you will, too. The dream will unfold before you in due time.

I wrote the vision. "When I grow up, I will be a teacher, then own my very own etiquette school. I will do commercial scriptwriting and I will own my own business and non-profit. I will travel the world and I will have a home in a few states." I remind my siblings about this statement constantly.

I learned at an incredibly young age that my words would manifest and give life to the very things I desire. I didn't hold myself short of choosing to live the life of my dreams. What I saw for myself was beyond my current situation. I knew that when it's not seen, it only takes faith and hard work, and then it will manifest. I held the desires before me and continued the path that would bring me success.

I mixed faith with work and started to volunteer in my community. I was unknowingly recognized by Warner Brothers, thanks to my counselor, Dr. Karen McEwen, for my outstanding commitment to community service. I was offered the opportunity to do a commercial as an acknowledgement of my service. Although the commercial opportunity was in front of the camera, it gave me the fuel I needed to know that, one day, I would be writing on the other side. Shortly thereafter, I graduated from high school in the top ten of my graduating class of over 160 students.

I attended Northwood University, a private four-year university. I majored in advertising, marketing and business management with a minor in English Language Arts, mathematics and logistics. Afterwards, I returned to complete my master's degree in secondary education. Teaching is where my heart was, but I knew the salary of a teacher wouldn't line up with my goals. I had to use my business education to start, open, and operate a profitable business.

> *"Write the vision and make it plain*
> *so the one that reads it can run with it."*
> – Habakkuk 2:2

In college, it seemed like every semester we had to write some type of business plan, complete financial forecasting and create vision boards. I understood that if you have goals, you also have to project how you will get to your destination, and these were all tools to assist.

Writing the vision is not just for you. When it comes to business, if you need others to assist in the operations, they must know where you're headed. With the energy of two or more people, you can do things much quicker. If you are in charge, you must have a vision for your team; but even outside of work, you must have a vision for yourself, your family, finances, health, education, extracurricular activities, and volunteering. Write it down!

Needless to say, many things that I once envisioned have come to pass and others I still wait on the manifestation. I am reminded every day when I rise to look at the vision for my life and for my future, and I take steps toward my goals! When you get witty ideas, write them down, fit them in, and one day your dream will make someone's life easier. Work on the vision daily, always allow yourself to dream. My beautiful child, write the vision.

POTENTIAL MEETS PURPOSE

Dear Destiny,

Potential is what you have the ability to do. Once it collides and unifies with your purpose on earth, together they form your destiny. Through education, you become informed; you begin to find your purpose and your purpose opens doors. If you were exposed to nothing, you can only dream about nothing; but when you see it and there's potential, it makes it possible to seize it.

We've talked about finding your way and passion, and I believe I've found mine. As a child, I knew that working with people was something I enjoyed because I deeply loved community, conversation, and the continuous roar of laughter in my household. I must admit that it was much later in life when it all clicked together, and I had the "A-ha!" moment. And the timing was perfect. Sometimes, you must arrive at a mature destination before your purpose is revealed so you don't sabotage your own success.

For many young people, their purpose is wrapped in talents discovered during adolescence. When their potential meets opportunity, doors open and create a smooth transition to the next level. For others, it takes years or an unexpected event for them to link up with their purpose.

For example, since my nephew Derrick was four years old, he strung lyrics together and only desired instruments for birthdays and Christmas. He was destined for the music industry—not surprisingly since my grandfather was a musician. Derrick worked hard daily. He would swiftly complete homework and chores so he could run back to his music and put pen to paper to capture the lyrical thoughts that ran through his head. He found his passion early and worked diligently to master his craft by age 21.

To find your purpose, you must be *you*—an authentic, unapologetic *you* who strives for greatness while bringing your flaws to the table as well. There is no room to copy anyone else. You can take the same path Oprah took and still not have her success because the variables and timing are not the same. Oprah has to be Oprah; therefore, you must set goals that work for you. Never leave your life vacant to live someone else's life. If you are "her," who will be "you?" It's important to be your own unique self, flaws and all. The fact that you continue to move forward is a testament of your strength.

The most amazing benefit of growing has to be the seeds you carry within, and the knowledge you gain on your path. Once the knowledge is gained, even if you grow out of your natural habitat or surroundings, like a flower, you can be replanted. You can transition to a new place with a solid foundation and great soil and grow again. Begin to take root and grow where you are planted. Start right where you are!

Once you find yourself, know the power you possess. That will help you arrive at your purpose. You have been given the power to love, the power to think, the power to believe, the power to have faith and the power to overcome. Pull on the power that you possess! The most dangerous thing you could ever do is turn that power over to another individual. It's been given to you so you can carry out your purpose and push the limits.

Ask yourself the following questions to exercise your thinking and acquire a better idea of where you're headed:

What am I good at?

What could I be good at?

What places near me offer opportunities that I can take advantage of?

How can I help make this world a better place?

Who do I love to see thriving?

What qualities do I love to express?

When am I happiest?

Where do I want to be in 10 years?

Start to live your life with purpose.

LETTER 8
SEIZE THE MOMENT

Dear Destiny,

I have just taken a long flight back from Paris.

My flight made a connection in New York and then on to Detroit. As always, I looked for my safe place—the Delta Lounge! The lounge was a ghost town with only the employees and maybe two to three guests making their way to grab a bite to eat. While I gazed through the soup options looking for the Wicked Thai Chicken & Wild Rice Soup, a small-statured African American woman walked into the lounge. I was already prepared to speak; I live to speak and make meaningful connections when it's appropriate. Lo and behold, that was the day I met Ms. Anita Baker, an amazing music icon and living legend.

In a calm voice, I told her how much my parents loved her music, and how this friend and that friend loves her, and how this cousin mimics her. She stopped me mid-sentence and taught me one of the most valuable lessons I would ever learn.

"This opportunity you have received is for no one else but you. I recognize the type of person you are because you've spoken so highly of everyone else; but tell me this: Who's out there doing the marketing for you? I want to know more about you. Let's take this moment and get to know the individuals that are present in this space."

Yeah, it pretty much blew my mind!

What was most interesting is that we didn't talk about music. She was so kind and wanted to know more about who I was and the ventures I took part in. I proceeded to tell her of the passion I have for the youth and the importance of empowering them with the knowledge of etiquette. I asked her about her thoughts on training girls in etiquette and she replied, "Etiquette opens doors, much like the doors that have been opened for you; you've been given access."

After much excitement, I had an "A-ha!" moment. I must admit I was a bit delayed in catching the revelation of the lesson she taught me. I was so grateful when it clicked, and I fully understood. She was simply saying that when it's your time to dance, give it your all. Be authentic. You are enough—take your time, shine and seize every opportunity. You deserve your moment.

"If you have any questions or if you want to sit and talk to me, I will be right here," Ms. Anita said at the conclusion of our conversation.

When you get a moment with Ms. Anita Baker, as my mom says, "Don't overstay your welcome." I sat near the food bar and mentally took in the moment. Later, I went to the gate to board my flight, only to run into Ms. Anita Baker again, who was on the same flight. There were only two people behind her on the jet bridge, then me. When she turned and saw me, she said, "There's my girl." I fainted twice on the inside; but outwardly, I smiled, and we continued with small talk, including those around us until we took our seats.

When I finally touched down from "Cloud 9"" – and from approximately 39,000 feet– I thought, *Wow, this is such a "God moment."* One of the greatest vocalists of all time carved out a moment to listen to me. What was even more amazing is that I really suffered from not really seeing myself. I understood and acknowledged everyone else's awesomeness except my own. I had to know and understand that what I brought to the table was good enough. I am worthy of love, and my truth is enough. Initially, I thought I was practicing humility; but in this case, it was actually not knowing that I should place myself first. If I could just save myself first, then I could open a door for so many others to have access.

Willis AirLines

BUSINESS CLASS   BOARDING PASS

NAME OF PASSENGER

(Place Your name here)

Flight   Date   From   Destination
A612   June 12, 2022   JFK

Boarding time   Gate   Seat Number
07:30am   B27   1B2

Departure time
08:00am

FRNS 128 1635748654656
SEQ 0004

Willis AirLines

NAME OF PASSENGER

Flight A612   Date June 12, 2022

From JFK

Destination Choose Your Destination

Boarding time Gate
07:30am   B27

Seat Number
1B2

Departure time   SEQ
08:00am

Willis AirLines

Thank you
for choosing Our Airline today.

Please be at your departure gate
at the indicated boarding time.

Any passenger failing to do so may
be refused boarding privileges.

Have a pleasant flight.

LETTER 9
BE HUMBLE

Dear Destiny,

Humility can take you so far. Let me share this story with you from my heart.

Ray and Piper were close friends who spent a lot of time to-gether throughout their middle and high school years. They lived in the same neighborhood, but their parents were in two, totally different tax brackets. Let's just say that Ray's family was rich, and Piper's family was poorer than all the surrounding families.

Piper shared everything with Ray – her secrets, struggles, her fears and even funny family stories of her cousins who lived just past the train tracks, who were dubbed "pure drama." Ray loved everything about Piper's life. Although he was privileged, he ad-mired how Piper worked diligently at her afterschool job at the local diner. Her report card never saw a B, and she was confident that she would grow up and establish her own business. Everyone else's future looked promising – not to mention the businesses the other kids will inherit from their rich families. And yet, Piper was starting from scratch.

Fast-forwarding a bit, they went on to college. Ray nestled right into the role he was born into – CEO of his family's security IT company. However, Ray never forgot Piper. After not seeing her at their 20-year class reunion, he decided to reach out through social media to see where she was hiding. Ray opened the search engine and typed, "Piper Goodman." He found she wasn't hiding at all. Ray spoke to her through social media, and the two began to chat back and forth:

> Ray: Long time, no see, stranger.
> Piper: Hey there, it's been forever. How's the family?
> Ray: Good, but most importantly, how are you? Are you living here in the city?
> Piper: I'm great thanks for asking and yes.
> Ray: Where are you working these days?
> Piper: Currently out of work but life is still looking up. No, really, I'm good.
> Ray: Please don't tell me...we all know "still looking up" is a cover up :-(
> I will have my driver pick you up so we can meet for lunch.

Piper always knew Ray had her back, although she never allowed him to prove it.

Throughout the years, Piper had made great strides in low-income communities and her career until one cold Detroit day. The contract she'd been working came to an end and she was out of a job. And it was nearly impossible to find another with how things were going within the economy. Piper started a cleaning business just to ensure she could make ends meet for her family, but she still struggled to keep things together.

Ray and Piper finally caught up, however, and after many old stories, new stories and laughs, Ray spoke up.

"See, Piper, what you have can't be bought. You've got spirit, joy, and just an incredible will to do what's right and succeed regardless. I probably would have folded if I was out of work. I would be so honored if I could help you and you could help me."

Piper shifted to catch up with the new mood. "What, really, could I do for you?" Ray scrolled down his phone contact list to share a contact with Piper.

"Call Divine Dawson tomorrow," Ray said. "With our company's expansion, we could use a great logistics team, especially if it's led by you." Things turned around for Piper pretty quick.

I learned so much from Piper's story; I hope you did as well. You're the CEO (Chief Executive Officer) of the future company you will own and oversee. One of the greatest attributes you can have is humility. Having an attitude of gratitude. Life has a way of turning the tables. It pays to treat people well whether you are climbing the ladder of success or descending for a season of reassessment. No matter the position you play in life, do it in excellence. Treat everyone well no matter what your or their status because what you give out will return. We hope if we ever find ourselves in need, a recompense of good would happen across our path.

Humility is *not* begging people to allow you to be the amazing person God placed you on this earth to be. Humility is letting your light shine while being conscious of those around you who are dim. Humility is offering to lead others to the supply source. It's knowing your worth and yet still, at the proper time, reaching out to consider those who are of a lower estate. You can be fierce *and* humble!

I've learned that people will forget what you said, people will forget what you did, but people will never forget how you made them feel.
– Dr. Maya Angelou

LETTER 10
DISCIPLINE

Dear Destiny,

There's so much going on around you that sometimes it's necessary to step away. It's necessary to shut out the noise for a moment and access where you are, where you want to be, and the path that will get you there. You may have to ask yourself a series of questions. It never hurts to "keep yourself in check." Remember, only you are responsible for *you*.

You must center yourself to get back into the rhythm that you were once stepping to. You must figure out if it's time to switch over to a totally new beat and walk that path. Whatever you choose to do, you must put together a plan and action steps. You must meditate on where you want to be and put the disciplines in place to get there.

Centering yourself is also necessary for your physical, mental and spiritual health. You can't be everywhere at one time; life requires decisions and habits that help you to stay on task.

Discipline and good habits can't be purchased. They don't come by desire; they are only met by *doing*. Every day, you have to do something, and some other days, you have to do a little more. You have to keep doing it until you form a habit. Ask yourself, "How bad do I want it?" However, also know the "why" behind what you want.

Have you ever taken advice from someone to join a program or a team? You have little interest in it, but you continue to do it because you've gotten into the habit of doing it. When you really think about it, it doesn't make you happy. It doesn't add any joy to your life, and it's not beneficial for your future. This is a great time to reassess.

Habits are formed through repetition. Habits are a part of your routine. Good habits include healthy eating, drinking lots of water, healthy conversation, good exercise, being grateful and a positive attitude. Manners are habits as well! Always remember to say, "Excuse me" when necessary, as well as "please" and "thank you." Good manners go a long way.

The strong attributes that you now possess through good habits will help you on your way to waking up to healthy habits in as little as two months, when building these prominent behaviors in your life.

Phillippa Lally is a health psychology researcher at University College London. According to a study published in the *European Journal of Social Psychology*, Lally and her research team took the initiative to research how long it actually takes to form a habit. Many were content with the former study done in 1961 by Maxwell Maltz, a plastic surgeon who stated that it takes a minimum of 21 days to develop a habit. The word "minimum" was done away with and the world ran with 21 days.

A new study was done that stated that it takes eight weeks minimum to form a new habit. It takes just over two months for behaviors to develop as automatic and from 18 to 254 days to form a new habit. The researchers discovered that if you, for any reason, missed a day, it wouldn't place a negative impact on forming that specific habit. The great thing is that you're young, and time is on your side. However, we must make the most of it and squeeze the opportunity out of each day while giving yourself permission to miss a day here and there. Start to set new habits based on where you see yourself in the future. Take yourself seriously if no one else does and go for it.

Good self-discipline helps you to prepare yourself for the real world.

Here are a few habits that will add value to your *amazing* life:

- Once your eyes open, meet that moment with gratitude. *You are alive!* Start by telling God, "Thank You".
- Smile.
- Laugh. Laughing releases endorphins, or "feel-good chemicals".
- Let the sunshine in.
- Breath in love, happiness, peace and joy; then breath out stress, distractions, disappointment, fear and regrets.
- Stand up straight.
- Stretch.
- Brush your teeth.
- Exercise or go for a walk.
- Keep a gratitude journal. Jot down a few things/people you're grateful for.
- Play and Speak your Affirmations.
- Drink water before each meal.

- Eat breakfast; choose vegetables over sugar.
- Compliment someone today.
- Give a gift today, no matter how small.
- Introduce yourself to someone new.
- Make great eye contact.
- Learn something new. Read and Listen.
- Check in with a life coach, mentor, accountability partner or teacher.
- Give a hug.
- Spread good manners such as "excuse me," "Please" and "Thank You" often.

INTEGRITY

*Manners may open the door, but integrity
will allow you access throughout the place.*

Dear Destiny,

Integrity is so important to me. I understand that people can surprise me and do the unthinkable, but I still like to believe that the world is not as bad as it seems. I like to believe that some people can still be trusted. Can I trust you?

Throughout my 16 years of teaching, I've never had students steal from me. Any student I taught knew there were a few key concepts we always had to cover:

- Respect yourself.
- Treat others like you want to be treated.
- Respect others, their property, and their personal space.

It's not about your behavior when people are watching, but more so your behavior when you are alone. It's important to train yourself to control your thoughts and actions. Think about the importance of not letting yourself down. You deserve to be invited in; even a person who's a stranger to you would even suggest you are "welcome to stay."

If you're in an empty room in a house and there was $500 on the floor, what would you do? You have a few options but know this first: if it's not your house, it's not your money. If you didn't lose any money, it's not your money until you've gone through the proper protocols to return it to its rightful owner and haven't succeeded. Where is the host or the person who invited you? You can let them know that someone dropped money.

I was the youngest of my parents' six children. We also had two amazing half siblings, Chris and Sonja, who lived many hours away. My mom trained us from an early age, teaching us to never take what wasn't ours and to ask for help if we needed something. My parents would leave money around the house and we knew not to touch it. We were taught to save, but we could still use that money to our discretion.

Side note: We would shake our piggy banks furiously when the ice cream truck came. I'm laughing on the inside just thinking about it! We still had to practice restraint because besides the ice cream truck, the fruit truck, the carnival truck, and the soft-serve truck also came down the street throughout the day.

Somehow, the discipline was there. Somehow, we grew up with eight people, three bedrooms and a lower level, a house full of children and friends, with balance and integrity. We could go over anyone's house because people knew and understood how we had been raised. We knew not to walk in without being invited in, and we knew not to open someone's refrigerator *ever*.

There are also safety precautions against friends, acquaintances, and guests walking around a house without supervision.

This is not the same in every home. Some homes don't have a standard set of rules and you are free to roam around; but when in doubt, just remember the standards mentioned.

Having integrity is amazing, but the extent of trust you give out must be coupled with wisdom. Only trust people in an area they don't suffer in. For example, if a person suffers with being a kleptomaniac (taking things impulsively), don't leave things around to tempt this person. Keep the person in a safe, theft-free environment, such as on the porch.

If a person takes embarrassing pictures without your permission or knowledge to post on social media later, watch yourself around them. If an individual lies often and twists the truth, limit your conversations with them. Always be kind, even when you have to dismiss yourself.

Etiquette requires integrity. Companies need individuals with integrity to do business with. When you collaborate, you represent yourself and their brand. Do things sincerely, and without malice. Daughter, please don't leave without the tools that will take your life to the next level. General education is not enough. You can have the intellect and the beneficial information that would be an asset to even NASA, but without an open door and integrity, you will never be able to show up to display your gifts. How you treat others says a lot about yourself and what you've been taught. And now that you know, you're left without any excuses.

LETTER 12
CHOOSE YOUR HAPPINESS

I have decided to stick with love. Hate is too great a burden to bear.
– Dr. Martin Luther King, Jr.

Dear Destiny,

Some days, I just don't feel pretty or happy. I'm not talking about an external look, but more so a feeling stemming from the inside – an emotion. The first thing I do is ask myself, *"Where is this coming from? What happened? How did I get here?"* But no matter what I do today, it's just not working out. I can't get it together nor find any relief. My first step was to acknowledge my feelings and never let my mood dictate my manners. If my feelings are out of control, I take the initiative to distance myself to avoid unintentionally hurting someone I love.

I woke up today totally not feeling it, and the first thing that came into my mind was: "Do it anyway."

Eat breakfast, read my morning devotion, recite my positive daily affirmations, and to remember that no one has the power to make me feel better more than myself. So, I did that. I persevered through the grogginess, fighting for yesterday's feelings of waking up happy, or at least not like this.

Mood Swings Happen

I went into work smiling yet appearing as if I missed an entire night of rest. After all, there's definitely a difference between sleep and rest. As if my day wasn't going badly enough, my coworker Donna greeted me with some devastating news that her best friend had been in a terrible car accident two days ago. I comforted her the best I could by offering her my ear and very few words.

Emotions

Donna told me they had been best friends since middle school. They'd graduated together, wore the same color to prom and had stories that would last them for years to come. You could feel the safety and warmth of the friendship just by listening to her sweet words. Right as she spoke, a light bulb went off.

"When do you return to visit her?" I asked. She responded by saying she would go home, get things in order with her husband and children, and then be at the hospital for the remainder of the day.

I encouraged Donna that when she got the opportunity to sit beside her friend and hold her hand, to tell her every story she could remember. I told her to speak about how hard they laughed together, cried, ran, walked, how she witnessed her friend's bravery and how she triumphed through every struggle.

"You become her strength!" I said. "Tell her of her future, tell her what you see!"

We departed to begin our assigned task and lead our teams to another successful third quarter closing. Donna's friend's health and recovery stayed on my mind. I offered small prayers throughout the day and checked on Donna to make sure she was holding up well. My "bad day" truly passed over because often our pettier issues pale in comparison to those who are facing real hardships.

In the days that followed, I continued to check on Donna and ask for updates. The process went a little slower than I imagined, but full recovery was the final result. Donna brought back a message from her friend:

Hi Sha'Malia,

Donna told me how you were her rock as she cared for me in such a difficult time. She came to the hospital every day and loaded me up with positive thoughts and future events that we would attend, as well as loads of things we would do. I just want to let you know that your faith is contagious, and not only did it motivate me to get up, but I'm sure you've noticed a change in Donna for the best. Thanks again for the prayers and support.

– Inga

Some days, you can be met with emotions that you were never introduced to. These emotions can come from a number of issues. Your body could possibly be tired, or you may have a lot on your mind. Whatever it is, we must find a way to manage our emotions on a day-to-day basis. There are many ways to do this, but first things first: You must be aware of the moment when you feel yourself going down. If you can't fight it or have no strength, just find a quiet space and take a moment for yourself.

The more you live, the more 'you will be able to get in touch with your emotions. Emotions are not always attached to mood swings. Sometimes, the loss of a loved one can put us in an emotional space. Different events trigger the emotion. It's healthy to find safety in family and friends and release these emotions through talking. Let the tears flow so you don't bottle it all up. Grief, in my opinion, is one of the strongest emotions that lifts in its own time. We will talk more about this in the near future.

Life is a series of ups and downs. Most days, you can see them coming; other days, like Donna's, they will take you by surprise. Either way, this world needs you.

I'm so grateful Donna was there for her friend. Who is your "safe person?" Who is the person you can call on to come to your aid without delay? We all need a "safe person." If you currently have that "safe person," remember to say, "Thank you."

Happy   **Sad**   **Relaxed**

Disappointed   **Angry**   **Cool**

LETTER 13
SOCIAL GRACES

Dear Destiny,

My mom has always been hilarious when it comes to these questions that she had concerning my friends. Picture coming home from school and inviting one of your friends over with the permission of all parents. Once you get into the house, your friend makes a mad dash to the couch. She throws down her wraps and backpack and leaves her shoes in the middle of the floor. This same friend then goes into the kitchen and opens the refrigerator to find herself a snack while casually holding a conversation.

I immediately flashback to my middle school teacher, Ms. Carson, asking, "Have you no home training?"

My mom would smile from ear to ear at my friend; however, she would always quietly ask me the questions I never had the answer to: "Who raised her? Who said she could go in the refrigerator? When did she move in?" (Side note: My mom understood, after moving from the South, that all families are not created equally. She would never judge you on something she had never taught you.)

It always made me chuckle so hard. My mom wouldn't dare be mean to my friends, but she made things quite clear to her children. We were definitely responsible for our company. So, let me rewind this story a bit and tell you where we both went wrong.

Whenever you go to anyone's house, there are a set of rules that you may have no idea about, and that's totally okay; but when in doubt, *ask*. My dear friend should've never run-in front of me. As a guest, you follow the host or the person who invited you over. My friend also shouldn't have put her things down on the couch. She should've asked where she could place her backpack, coat, and shoes. Going even further, it was my duty to beat her to the questions and let her know the unwritten rules for our home. Concerning my upbringing, we were taught to not go into anyone's refrigerator. It should've gone more like this:

As we walk through the door, I would say, "We are so happy to have you over, feel free to get comfortable. If you need anything, just ask. Your coat goes here in the front closet, along with your shoes. Feel free to bring your backpack along with you since we will be studying later. I will grab some snacks and something to drink from the refrigerator; you can have a seat on the couch. Should you need to use the bathroom, it's the second door on your right. If you need anything else, just let me know."

This does not mean my guest was not free to stand up, sit down and twirl if she wished. These are just guidelines I should've given her so she would've known what's expected and where she could find everything within our home. Sometimes, depending on how many times the person has visited, we would say, "Make yourself at home; you know where everything is."

Researchers from a study based on results from 126 university students that's published in *Social Psychological and Personality Science* found evidence that a single glance of a person's face for just 33 to 100 milliseconds was sufficient to form a first impression.

Your first impression is an indelible mark that typically never goes away once you've been present in someone's life. How great it would be if you always make that moment memorable in the best way. Be on time, preferably fifteen minutes early. Strolling in at the exact time makes you late since the ball is already rolling. Always be ready to learn, and in order to do that, you must come prepared to listen. Even if you don't agree with them, remember to respect their time and position, as they also respect your time and position. You only get one time to make a first impression, so make it count!

Appearance is crucial as well; always make sure you look the part. After all, you never know when an opportunity will sneak up on you. People buy into what you have more quickly if you're presentable. Don't slouch! Remember how important posture is. There's not much to say when your body language is doing so much talking.

You want your presence to say, "I'm happy to meet you. I'm honest and trustworthy. You have my attention; you will be grateful that you've met me," all while initially saying nothing. Nonverbal communication must only give off positive vibes. When you speak, be sure to watch your tone; you should always sound pleasant and attentive. Do understand that you are an asset to any relationship or organization.

Social graces are needed for social situations. Developing the skill set of being polite during interaction can open doors for future relationships, job opportunities, and the like. Proper deportment, manners, and etiquette are the epitome of social graces.

POSTURE & GREETINGS

Dear Destiny,

When you walk into any room, it is most important to greet and/or acknowledge those who make eye contact with you. If the room is large, then a warm smile goes a long way. If the room is small, it's equally important to quietly say hello to those who are near you and make eye contact. If a couple of people are in attendance, greet them each individually by a formal introduction from the host or yourself. This is all dependent upon the engagement. The following is an example of how to make your introductions.

> *Sha'Malia: Hello, my name is Sha'Malia and it's a pleasure to meet you.*
> *(The other individual should give you their name in return. If not, it's okay.)*
> *Sha'Malia: And your name is?"*
> *New Person: Cordon.*
> *(Repeat their name to ensure you got it correct before going to the next person)*
> *Sha'Malia: Cordon, again it's a pleasure.*

There is also a proper way to introduce your friend to your parents or another superior. Always introduce the older person first.

Sha'Malia: Dad, this is my friend, Medina. Medina, this is my Dad.
Dad: Medina, a pleasure to meet you.
Medina: Pleased to meet you as well, Mr. Willis.

When addressing an adult or dignitary, always place a form of address before a person's name unless they ask you otherwise. For example: Ms., Mr., Dr., Your Honor, Her Excellency, etc. A hand is often extended during the introduction. A firm, friendly handshake is no more than two to three pumps. Never squeeze their hand during the handshake!

Please and Thank You

"Please" and "Thank You" are words that often open doors. Kind words often results in generous responses, so the golden rule still stands: *Do unto others as you would have them do unto you.* Merely treat people the way you want to be treated.

If, for any reason, you have to reach over someone, remember to say, "Pardon my reach."

Posture

Posture is the ability to use the correct muscles to hold your body up straight while sitting, standing or even lying down. Good posture sharpens your look. Posture is important; so, sit up straight, please. Good posture is also associated with good health and longevity. Good posture relates to the activity of your limbs, great alignment, prevention of arthritis, and backaches. Always research the correct lifting positions if you ever have to lift anything heavy.

Coughing and Sneezing

Should you feel the need to excuse yourself while at the table or standing within a group of people in conversation, say, "Excuse me, please." Excuse yourself if you start coughing or sneezing excessively. There's an appropriate way to both cough and sneeze in public. If there is tissue available, sneeze or cough into the tissue and dispose of it in a wastebasket. If there is no tissue available, cough or sneeze into your upper sleeve. Never cough or sneeze in your hand; the visual alone makes people not want to shake your hand ever again.

Every good and bad conversation must come to an end. Always close a conversation out instead of abruptly walking away. Close the conversation with, "It was great talking with you," or "Nice catching up with you," and the like.

Social graces are important because you never know who could be an open door for your next level or next chapter. People may not remember the exact words spoken, but they often remember how you made them feel.

MIND YOUR MANNERS

"Good manners are just a way of showing
other people that we have respect for them."
– Bill Kelly, Blast from the Past, 1999

Dear Destiny,

"Grace, have you no home training?" asked my sixth-grade teacher, Ms. Carson. "Feet out of baskets," she would say. Not all of us understood that she meant to take your feet off the furniture. Etiquette is the behavior you display when you speak to your neighbor, when you hold the door for the individual behind you, or when you allow the rows of people on the plane to deplane or exit in front of you. Etiquette displays patience and is equivalent to respect. It shows kindness and courtesy to those you come in contact with.

I am truly fortunate to have parents from the south. "Southern Hospitality" always ensured that visitors received good treatment from us. When my parents moved to the Midwest, they brought their hospitable manners right along with them. These manners included "please," "thank you," "excuse me," and being courteous, all of which I teach my students.

If you came to our house, you could sit at the table, eat with us and make yourself feel at home. We knew it was a southern thing because my friend's parents weren't like that.

Etiquette has a lot to do with your upbringing and it's often spoken through your actions. This information is important to know, and it's my job to teach you that when you go out, you not only represent yourself, but those who taught you.

I desire to teach you everything that will open many doors of opportunities and place you amongst the most influential leaders. From there, you will have the tools to adjust the temperature in any room when you walk in.

Poise is also a part of etiquette. It's how you carry yourself, how you walk into a room, completely sure of yourself, with your head held high and a warm smile on your face. Poise is humility with grace, not boisterous, pompous pride. Being sure of yourself is not looking down on others; it's being certain of yourself.

Etiquette should start at home; however, as an international educator, I know the kind of etiquette taught and learned can vary from house to house. Not everyone possesses good manners. Because etiquette is slowly becoming a "lost art" within this generation, its rarity will allow you to stand out amongst the crowd.

Etiquette is an unspoken, necessary protocol. It's polite to step back so that others can go before you. This concept is not to belittle yourself; if anything, it's the opposite. Etiquette is far from an "eye for an eye" kind of attitude. Those who will reward you for it typically have more status and ability to open doors of opportunity for you. It plays a hand in "karma" – what you put out will come back.

Imagine going to your first job interview and not holding the door for the person right behind you only to later find out that

that person is the one who's interviewing you. Not holding the door doesn't make you a bad person but holding the door does say to the person behind you that you're thinking about more than just yourself. And that's a valuable benefit in any large corporation.

Etiquette for me started at a young age. I was very rough around the edges and didn't understand that there was a time and place for everything. I had to hear the truth again and again until I understood how beneficial it was for me. It all started with participating in Girl Scouts in elementary school, soon followed by a session of etiquette at church taught by Debbie Winans-Lowe. We learned what to order and what messy dishes not to order while dining formally. Though small, this experience stayed with me for a lifetime.

I was polite, but full of energy. I felt like no one would be bothered with me dancing around all day, even during class. Looking back on it now, it's quite laughable. My music teacher, Mrs. Gay, told me that I should consider trying out for the dance and majorette team. She went on about how my energy would be put to good use there. I tried out and I made both teams. There was a place for me to display my gift and release my energy.

This same teacher played a great part in my upbringing. She pointed me toward the French Club, modeling, volunteering, teaching and more. I had so much energy that these extracurricular activities were only few of many. The greatest encouragement she offered was to become a member of the most illustrious sisterhood, Delta Sigma Theta Sorority, Inc.! Mrs. Gay played an extremely important role in my life.

Etiquette became a passion as I pursued my extracurricular activities. I had a yearning to learn more about it. I've always loved learning how to do something the "right way," if there's a right way to do it. So, I found out there was a proper way to place the napkin, to sip the tea and to twirl the fork. That all amazed me, and I was hooked from the beginning.

Although I have a great passion for etiquette, and I have an even greater passion to see you succeed and go far in life. I love sharing this wisdom with you. I just want you to be informed and seize every opportunity. No matter what, you will have to walk this path yourself; but being equipped will take you so far and much faster.

LETTER 16
GOT WISDOM?

Dear Destiny,

These first few weeks are a little difficult because the focus is only on *you*. *No* pointing the finger, no blaming – but just taking full control of the decisions you make from here on out.

The wisdom I share is connected to the wisdom of the masses.

When I write these words, they are not just my own. It's over 30 years of teaching from names to numerable to count. Great teachers like Bishop Elect Marvin L. Winans, years of learning and teaching in the classroom, studying under great professors at universities, years of studying under Dr. Cindy Trimm, years of volunteering at our local girls' club, at the girl's home and speaking with youth and reading countless books. I received encouraging wisdom of those I've studied– Dr. Maya Angelou, Shirley Chisholm, Dr. Dorothy Height, Oprah Winfrey, Nelson Mandela, Lee Kuan Yew, Og Mandino and countless others.

I study the greats – those who took the path less paved and overcame many obstacles so I would be able to stand upon their stable shoulders. The greatest thing to ever guide my life is *wisdom*. According to Merriam-Webster, *wisdom* is the quality of having experience, knowledge, and good judgment. That's exactly what I've obtained by allowing wisdom to lead me.

The Bible says that, "Wisdom is the principal thing" (Proverbs 4:7). You can't make the best decisions without it. Have you ever wondered, "Why did I have to go through this?" or "Why was I subjected to that?" Even though we don't always immediately know the "why," we do know that you can find a lesson in every single situation. Whether it be, "I would never do that again," or "life is not always fair," or "some people can't be trusted," or "I deserve better," know that all things will work together to produce goodness in your life.

The Wisdom to Study

Wisdom is the revelation of knowledge. The things we go through give us wisdom for future situations. Sometimes, it's to help others. Failing a test, for example, can have many effects, such as your grades dropping or failing an entire grade level. However, when the next test is administered, with wisdom, you can decide to do something different so you can get a different result. Studying, this time, could get you a much better outcome.

I'm currently studying for a test, but there's no guarantee that I will answer each question correctly. 'But if I familiarize myself with the materials, my chances of excelling will be high. When you study for the test and pass, it shows that you possess knowledge. Not all tests are created equally; some skill levels are increasingly difficult even when studying, depending on your prior knowledge.

Sometimes, it's not just the content but the strategy of how you study. You don't want to over study and you *definitely* don't want to under study. You must develop study habits so that you can read, understand and explain the content.

Follow some of these study strategies to continuously gain better test results:

STUDY TIPS
- ☑ Set realistic goals
- ☑ Create a study schedule
- ☑ Create a distraction-free zone
- ☑ Focus to ensure you're comprehending the material
- ☑ Create flash cards
- ☑ Create practice quizzes
- ☑ Take breaks when needed
- ☑ Drink Water

Wisdom When Choosing Your Friends and Acquaintances

Choose friends who are going in the same direction you are. I know you possess great confidence and always pour the type of love in friendships that encourage your friends to go far. It's even good to choose friends who meet the same goals you envision. When you get new friends, don't smother them and let no one smother you. Enjoy friendship! Making demands and controlling who gets to be an individual's friend is taking too much control over someone's life.

There's a balance to friendship. There's also a difference between a friend and a parent. You don't want to hound your friends about what's right or wrong. You should be able to simply tell them and move on. If you are making no headway, let another intervene. We may have friends who struggle with addictions. You must allow professionals to intervene in some matters, as well as allow your friends to have their own consciousness and convictions concerning what is right or wrong.

Keep in mind that there is room for growth, so be patient. Leave room for non-judgmental falls and setbacks and encourage your friends to persevere. A listening ear does not always mean you need to lend advice, especially if it's the advice that your friend is fully aware of and not asking for.

Wisdom saves time. You need wisdom every single day so you can avoid repeating the same test. Spend your time wisely because you can't get it back.

Be Wise

Be wise as to whom or what you give your time.

Be wise; don't give in to peer pressure.

Be wise in your teaching; never argue with someone who's not interested in learning.

Perspective without wisdom is cheap advice.

Be wise and agree to disagree on whether the cup is half empty or half full.

Be wise with your spending habits.

LETTER 17

EDUCATION

Dear Destiny,

According to Wikipedia, "Education is the process of facilitating learning, or the acquisition of knowledge, skills, values, beliefs, and habits. Educational methods include storytelling, discussion, teaching, training, and directed research."

Stagnation is not an option. What you don't know can actually hurt you, even *kill* you. If you don't know that eating healthy leads to better odds of not developing illnesses, you could put yourself in harm's way. We have to be susceptible to knowledge to help us grow. Just like plants need sunlight and water for growth, we need wisdom and knowledge for the same thing.

School is so important, whether it be homeschooling, boarding school, private school, or local public school. You must value education and know the importance of learning. Understand how blessed you are to have access to an education. It only takes learning for you to become whatever you dream of.

What I love most about education is that part of the vision has already been created for you. There is always something to look forward to, even from a young age. You graduate kindergarten, looking forward to carrying on with the "big kids." You graduate elementary school, looking forward to a playground without swings, slides and monkey bars. Now it's time to intellectually stimulate your mind with conversation about the hottest Ivy Park gear and at what age your parents will allow you to dye the tips of your hair. Either way, this is currently a system you will navigate through until you graduate from high school.

This vision can be altered and attained either quickly or slowly. You may leap over some grades and others you may add a greater workload with college prep classes. For the most part, your primary and secondary component of education is laid out for you. This helps create a great foundational vision.

I remember when I thought I knew *everything*. After hitting seventh grade, I felt that I was ready for the world. I could use the toaster oven and could cook all the things I loved. I was doing great in school, helping in the middle school office, oftentimes after lunch. I volunteered after school with the elementary Girl Scouts for my niece, Da'Porschia. I was so good in math that my teacher, Mrs. Hopkins, challenged me to go to the board and show her step-by-step how I managed to complete my work so fast. She never felt intimidated; she only laughed and always gave me a shot at the board to show how I worked out each problem.

I felt like I was living my best life in middle school. Then, in no time at all, I was graduating from college and it was then I realized I didn't actually know anything about life. I was great at cooking with the microwave and toaster, but not the stove. Crossing the street was a breeze, but I still couldn't drive. When I did learn how to drive, suddenly I had the responsibility of car notes and insurance. I needed a reliable business or job.

All this time, I thought I was grown; yet, I didn't really have a clue about *anything*. There were two older women who would remind me that I was young and had yet to know much about life. Mother Willie Mae Sheard and Mother Ruth told me I had to "keep living." I didn't understand it then, but I totally understand it now.

Education is important, and learning is growth. There are many ways to learn besides in the classroom; there are books, e-books, and documentaries that offer a wealth of information. You will learn as you go, and life happens fast. You will learn how to handle situations differently as you mature. You'll learn that not everything deserves a response, as well as the power of forgiveness. Having knowledge puts you in a different league. It strengthens your intuition and discernment.

You can learn, grow, and prepare to be counted amongst the greats; or you can hang out with people who see "change" as a threat. You can study just enough to get by, or you can practice pitching in the major leagues. There are levels to this which you can choose. With my guidance, you'll have the support to go as far as you desire. You will excel, but preparation is key.

LETTER 18
YOUR FIRST JOB INTERVIEW

Dear Destiny,

Preparation is essential to better the odds of your outcome. When you attend your first job interview, there are a few things you should know so that you're prepared.

As a senior in high school, I had a computer technology class and a business class. Teaching those classes were two of the most amazing teachers in the building.

Mrs. Elaine Wilmore and Dr. Dedria Willis prepared us for future careers. We had to create resumes, which outlined background information as it pertained to our experience in specific areas of education, work, organizations, clubs, and core values. The resume helped the employer (the person hiring us) know whether or not we were a good fit for the job. We created our resumes and cover letters with Dr. Willis, and prepared for our mock interviews, making the proper edits with Mrs. Wilmore.

Our final project was the interview. We did everything possible to be at our best—not only for our grade, but to secure the job. We learned that, based on the company we wanted to work for, it was important to tailor our resumes to fit what they were looking for. The resume couldn't include everything we've ever done, but instead it highlighted a few things that would make us great candidates.

If you're applying for a job as junior counselor for a summer camp, your participation as president of the National Honors Society and a member of Junior Achievement might be the better choice for your resume versus your amazing cheerleading skills. It's a great sport; but the skills aren't really applicable to managing and supervising kids.

It's important to research the company you're applying at. Learn about the culture of the company. Read reviews about how they treat their employees and see how long they have been in business. Also, look for when the company was founded, and by whom. What needs are they trying to fulfill? Be sure to read over their mission statement multiple times. You must be knowledgeable about the product and services the company provides. Is this a short-term job, or do you actually see yourself being there and advancing into another position? Is there room for growth?

The Interview Questions
When interviewing, you must be prepared to answer a few common questions:

- Why do you believe you're a good fit for this job?
- Out of all the candidates, why should we hire you?
- What type of work environment do you like best?

Consider your answers and rehearse them. Be assertive, listen, and talk. Sell yourself during the interview, sounding confident but not arrogant and remember that you can be kind without being passive.

Key Attributes

What do you want them to know about you? Write down three key attributes that would make you most valuable for the position you are applying for. Give examples of how your leadership skills have been used and yielded a favorable outcome. Be sure to include problem-solving skills in your examples. Focus on your strengths but be prepared to include a weakness. You may be asked what your biggest weakness is. When answering, state that you make no excuses for it and you're working to improve in that area. Weaknesses may include something like being a workaholic or losing track of time.

Study Your Resume

Look over your resume multiple times. Make sure that it's authentic. If the interviewer asks you about something that's on the resume, you have to be quick to respond to "your truth."

Closing Interview Questions

What makes an ideal candidate for this job? How could I best prepare for the job before I start? When do you plan to make a hiring decision for this position? What hours are available (or expected) for this position?

Dress for Success

No matter what the job uniform calls for, you must dress professional for your interview. *Jeans, gym shoes or T-shirts should not be worn.* Wear nice, clean and pressed dress pants or a skirt, and a collared shirt.

Arrive Early

If your interview is at 1 p.m., arrive 15 minutes early and take a seat. You may not be seen just because you've arrived early. Oftentimes, there are other interviews still going on or wrapping up.

Remain Professional

When you greet the interviewer, you must continuously be *professional.* No matter how kind the interviewer is, he or she is not there to become friends with you. Make sure you thank the interviewer for their time and allowing you to interview. Maintain a positive attitude and avoid talking about your personal life.

Thank You Note

The next day, send a "Thank You" note to the interviewer, which is always a kind gesture. If you don't hear anything within 72 hours, feel free to follow up unless you were told differently during the interview. "When should I look to hear from you?" is a proper question to ask concerning follow-up.

It's safe to say that we worked hard on our interview skills, got the job, and passed the class. Learning these keys for success allows you to be chosen out of a crowd. I'm so grateful for the amazing teachers who taught us the life skills needed to secure jobs, allowing us to use our skills and expertise to succeed.

ETIQUETTE EVERYWHERE

"Etiquette is wisdom."
– Dr. Dorie McKnight

Dear Destiny,

I can't wait for us to take a trip to the Motherland (Africa) together. It's beyond what words could describe! The culture is so rich, and the diversity is so powerful. The afro-beats heard in the distance while leaving the airport was all the welcome I needed. The royal colorful garbs that draped behind each individual added visual music to each step.

I wondered with all the different conversations going on what everyone was talking about. The languages were innumerable, but most spoke English, which I was surprised to learn. Unfortunately, the stories they tell us on the television do not define the entire continent of Africa. It's beautiful there. I loved that the tribe protecting their own is not viewed as a threat. The food is also extraordinary!

Etiquette for Everything!

There are protocols for everything. This means that there's a proper way to do things. There's church etiquette, concert etiquette, school etiquette, tech etiquette, international travel etiquette, business etiquette, plane etiquette, classroom etiquette, and the list goes on. Oftentimes, these forms of etiquette include proper greetings, attire, and proper behavior in a given setting. With technology being readily available, you must know that there's a time when devices can't be used. For example, cell phone usage of any kind is prohibited when you're in line at Customs to depart or return to a given country.

Etiquette is not the same everywhere. For example, the way you hold a fork in America is not the same way it's done in Europe. So, if you should dine elsewhere, you must do your research to find out what's proper and what could be offensive. When in doubt, ask.

I was having dinner with a friend who had flown in from Europe. As we began to eat, I observed that she kept her fork in her left hand. I asked her if she was familiar with the forms of fork etiquette. The European style had the fork exclusively in the left hand, while the American style consisted of the fork shifting between left and right hands. Surprisingly, she wasn't familiar with the American style; she assumed that the European fork etiquette was universal.

Displaying etiquette allows you to place yourself in a humble position and to learn the importance of allowing others to promote you above you promoting yourself. Humility is taking a general seat and being invited to the front versus assuming that the front seat is available because it's not occupied. Etiquette is already within you, waiting to be awakened. Once you decide that this will be a way of life, everything else will line up and it will become second nature.

LETTER 20
FORMAL DINING ETIQUETTE

Dear Destiny,

Will just any fork do? Absolutely not!

Before you know it, you will be traveling the "friendly skies" and attending fancy dinners in Bali. You will sit amongst cultures and customs that you may never have known existed. As always, it's my duty and privilege to make sure you are equipped for those moments. I want you to know that *the fork matters*. There are two types of dining methods – informal and formal. Let's first talk about informal American style dining.

Informal dining speaks of more than just a meal. There's typically a casual atmosphere, and it can mean the difference between wearing jeans or a costume, to deciding between a hot dog and caviar on the menu. An informal dinner can include a themed-based event which is typically more laid back with an inviting tone. Informal dining is likened to casual dining, as formal dining is to fine dining. The courses typically include one to two courses, and they're moderately priced.

The cutlery and flatware are typically basic. Usually, reservations aren't necessary. Less formal food options include nacho bars, taco bars, burger stations, fajitas and tons of other options.

Formal dining is vastly different, and so are the expectations. There is first a *host/hostess*. This person typically invites people for the party or event. The *invitation* covers the date, time, and location, as well as any other pertinent information guests need to know. There may also be a *theme* for the event. The theme helps guests understand the proper attire to be worn. Remember, if it's a sit-down dinner, be very conscious of what top you choose to wear because during the meal, the only thing visible is the upper part of your body.

Posture is important. Always check your posture. Make sure you're comfortable. There is no dancing and singing at the formal dining table. To pass dishes and items, always offer to the person on the left before passing to the right. And remember to say, "Please" and "thank you."

RSVP

Invitations will always include the option to R.S.V.P. I ask a lot of people what they think it means, and they usually say something to the extent of "reserve a spot." While that's true, I want you to know exactly what it means.

R.S.V.P. is French for *Répondez S'il Vous Plaît,* which is translated into English as *Please Respond.* That's what the host wants you to do: *please respond.* Your response could be to agree to come (with a guest, as well, if the option is given) or you can send your regrets if you won't be able to attend. Either way, send it within the allotted time. When the host has a headcount, they can properly request the accommodations needed for their event, such as a venue, chairs, gift bags, food and a host of other things. So *please respond!*

A *host* is a person who receives or entertains other people as guests. The host is the one who invited you to their event. The host is the key player at any event. Always remember to follow the host. If *you're* the host, you're the instructor and must lead your guests. Show them the protocols associated with their visit. Remember to tell your guests where to sit or stand (if there are no name placements), where the restrooms are, and where to pick up their wraps (coats, scarves, etc.).

It's always acceptable to bring a gift for a birthday party or celebration. It's important to be on *time* if you are attending an event with a scheduled itinerary or performance. When entering the event, always *greet* the host properly. Look for your name in the seating if it's been arranged, and never switch or change name tags. Only when the *host* sits are you free to sit. Once the host begins to eat, feel free to follow along. Taste food before seasoning it; pass the salt and pepper together even if only one is requested.

Whose fork is it anyway? The funniest thing can happen if you don't understand place settings and the importance of where you can find your fork, or else you run the risk of "fork-napping" your neighbor's utensils. When everyone at the table is knowledgeable in dining etiquette, dinner should go much smoother. You must understand your place setting and which fork is used for which dish.

The place setting is the blueprint for a beautiful dinner. It gives you an outline of what is to come, such as how many courses will be served. All utensils are placed outside of the plate, and that placement is further decided by the order of use. The guest should use utensils starting from the outside inward. All utensils displayed will be in use at some point or another during the course of eating.

I can't tell you that everywhere you go, the napkin will be found in the same spot. You will typically find it either on the plate, just left of the plate or the waiters/waitresses will bring one to you. You must keep up with your napkin and use it strategically. Napkins are made to withstand dirt. However, the task is to keep the napkin's exposure to dirt as little as possible so that it always appears clean. When you finish eating, don't place your napkin on the plate. Don't ball up your napkin. Always fold the stained portion of the napkin inward to keep it from getting on your clothes or chair. Keep your napkin off the table until others have finished eating. Should you need to get up from the table, simply place your napkin on the chair.

Here's a quick method I came up with to remember which side the fork, spoon, and knife goes on. The ridges of the knife should be pointed toward the plate, directly next to the plate.

4 Letter Word	5 Letter Word
1-2-3-4	1-2-3-4-5
L-E-F-T	R-I-G-H-T
F-O-R-K	K-N-I-F-E
	S-P-O-O-N

Cutlery includes knives, forks, and spoons used for eating or serving food. There's a right way to use cutlery. Do you know how to properly eat with your fork and knife? The American method of eating with the fork and knife requires that you hold the knife in your right hand (assuming you're right-handed) to cut your food while your fork is held in your left hand. After your food is cut, the knife can be placed on your plate and the fork is now switched to the right hand with the tines facing upward to place the bite of food in your mouth.

Another great way to remember placement is remembering the letters "BMW": Bread, Meal, and Water. Look at the display below for reference.

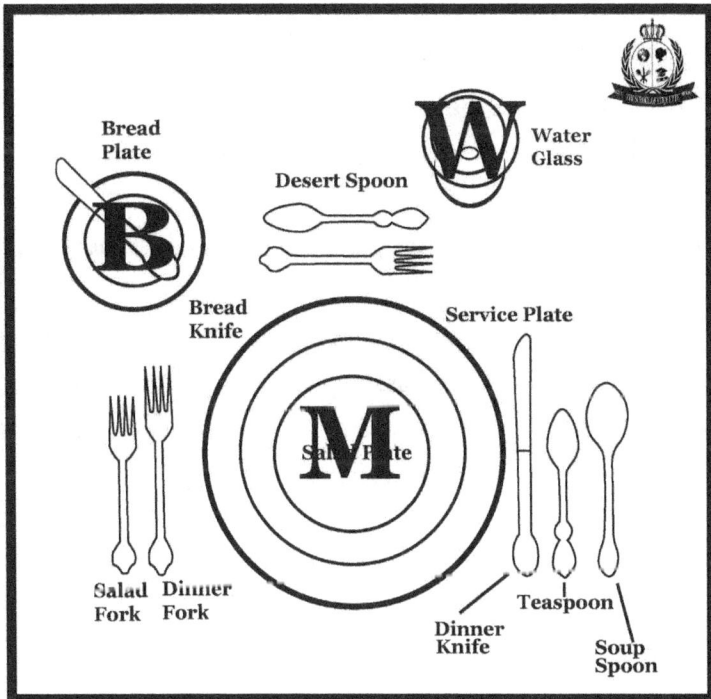

When eating soup, always dip the spoon outward, away from yourself to prevent splattering. Touch the spoon on the edge of the bowl to remove or avoid dripping. Scoop the soup away from the bowl to your mouth. Do not make slurping noises nor tip the bowl with your hand.

Etiquette Dining Tips

Think about the following finger foods: pizza, asparagus, zucchini sticks, bread, corn on the cob, and sandwiches. These are the foods that you can pick up and eat without using a fork. There are times when these foods aren't eaten with your fingers, such as when the food includes sauce or when it's too hot, greasy, or if it's overloaded with toppings. Hence, a fork is necessary.

If you're using chopsticks, don't stand your chopsticks upright in your rice or food; lay them flat on the table. When you are finished eating, place them flat on your bowl.

To butter your bread properly, use your butter knife and place butter on the side of your bread plate. Tear off one, bite-sized piece of bread at a time, and butter only that piece before eating it.

Do not drink with food in your mouth. Do not gulp. Lip gloss and/or lipstick should be carefully chosen to prevent smudging the glass. Also, it's not proper to crunch on the ice during dinner and never drink from a bottle in a formal setting.

Dining Etiquette

FORMAL

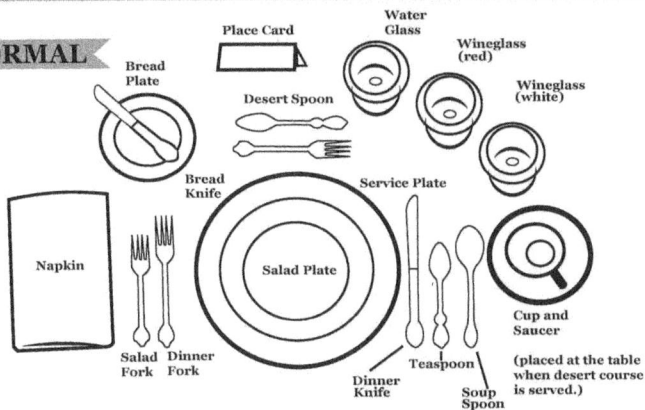

Place Card

Water Glass

Wineglass (red)

Wineglass (white)

Bread Plate

Desert Spoon

Bread Knife

Service Plate

Napkin

Salad Plate

Cup and Saucer

Salad Fork   Dinner Fork

Teaspoon

Dinner Knife

Soup Spoon

(placed at the table when desert course is served.)

INFORMAL

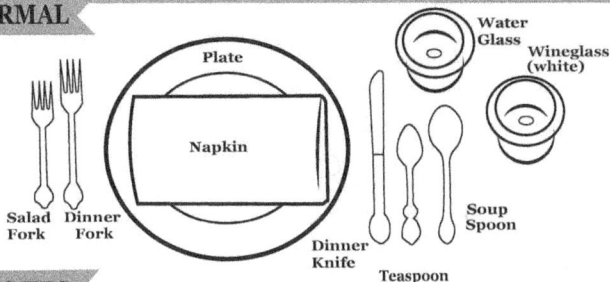

Plate

Water Glass

Wineglass (white)

Napkin

Salad Fork   Dinner Fork

Soup Spoon

Dinner Knife

Teaspoon

DINING TIPS

When eating soup, tilt the spoon away from you.

Eating Soup

Salt and pepper should always be passed together.

Salt & Pepper

Knives and forks should be held in a relaxed manner.

Holding Utensils

Resting

Finished

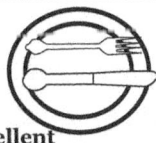

Excellent

85

WELCOME TO INTERNATIONAL ETIQUETTE

Dear Destiny,

The word, *etiquette*, is French for "ticket." Etiquette not only opens doors; it *grants you access*. You need a ticket to get into a ticketed event. To live amongst the greats, you need a ticket as well, but this ticket can't be scanned. Instead, it's woven into your very being. It's etiquette—your access ticket around the world.

International Etiquette will help you better navigate, stay safe, and in line with the customs, culture, and climate of different countries. As you travel the world, you will find that some people live very differently from us. It's a pleasure to learn about their history. We follow the rules of the world out of respect, while staying true to who we are. When it comes to understanding another culture and its customs, I truly consider it an experience.

There is a "way to be" in every part of the world, and different types of etiquette and protocols are expected. One of the most beautiful, serene countries I've ever been to is Singapore. I went during one of the most pivotal moments in the country's history, namely the state funeral of Prime Minister Lee Kuan Yew, who governed Singapore for three consecutive decades and essentially transitioned his country from the "third world to first world in a single generation" (DBPedia). You must take a moment to study his life and leadership in your near future. He had amazing *vision*.

Singapore is remarkably diverse. There, you can find people from all walks of life. Chinese, Malaysian, and Indian ethnic groups are the most dominant in the country. Singapore, in my opinion, has etiquette wrapped into every thread of the country's moral fabric; yet, the fabric represents the bridging of a plethora of cultures. When people think of etiquette, they often think of the proper way to eat or sit; but etiquette consists also of behaviors, mannerisms, and even boundaries. Let's talk about Singapore and China for a moment.

Singaporean Etiquette

When I flew into Singapore, I did not know what would meet me on the other side of the boarding door of the airbus. When I got outside the airport, it was a beautiful sight to behold. Singapore is full of colorful cultures from all over the world. However, Singapore is known for its strict rules and fines. There are protocols in place that must be followed, or else there are consequences to face.

For example, chewing gum was banned in efforts to keep the country of Singapore clean.

There are great reasons to enforce policies, especially when it will one day be mutually beneficial for all. Some fines must be paid for, like disobeying the laws. *You* are responsible for researching these things before travel. Here are a few things some do in everyday life that are not tolerated in Singapore:

Singapore "The Fine City"

Chewing Gum	$1,000 Fine
Feeding the monkeys	$250 Fine
Smoking	$1,000 Fine
Pets/Animals	$500 Fine
Littering	$1,000 Fine
Spitting	$1,000 Fine

Here's something you may already be comfortable with. Make sure you shake hands with everyone present at a meeting or social occasion. Singaporeans may bow slightly as they shake your hand. One thing I've noticed, being tall myself, is that many Westerners are generally taller than Singaporeans. So, it would be polite to give a small bow.

Chinese Etiquette

China was *amazing!* I had the time of my life there; but familiarizing myself beforehand with China's cultural practices only partially prepared me. I was extended a lot of grace because I didn't speak the language nor had I ever lived there. After skipping around the country, I can leave you with a few details for your trip.

Once you arrive (timely!) and take off your shoes before entering the house, you are halfway in their good graces. There is no need for a bow while greeting Chinese; a handshake with a smile will do the job. A simple *hi* or *ni hao* (meaning "hello") is how many Chinese people greet each other. You should greet the elderly with "ni hao." Always show up to a home with a small gift. Fruit baskets are great gifts (excluding pears). Abstain from giving sharp objects, clocks, and handkerchiefs. Sharp objects suggest that you want to cut or sever the relationship. If you're given a gift, always refuse the gift a couple of times before deciding to take it. If you receive the gift offered to you, save it to open later. Always receive what's given to you with both hands. Also, names are not written in red ink in Chinese society because names are written in red on gravestones.

We learned how to use chopsticks in one of our previous letters, but I didn't mention the pair of chopsticks in the center of the table. Known as *gong kuai* or public chopsticks, those never enter anyone's mouth. You use them to gather food from the serving tray, the same way we use the serving utensils in America.

If you're well-rounded and skilled in the art of international etiquette, you will enjoy your time in China and anywhere you go.

LETTER 22
LEARNING & TEACHING:
I BECAME THEM

Dear Destiny,

I have dedicated my life to providing you with the most valuable education I could give you: *wisdom*. That, in itself, is a gift we all wish we had been offered early on. Oftentimes, I'll say, "If I knew then what I know now, I would've made many different decisions." I'm giving you a head start, removing the excuses and the limits. It won't take away your life experiences, but the art of etiquette will certainly help you navigate your way through life.

Etiquette is not an option. It is an everyday necessity in a civilized world. Did you know that when an individual is comfortable and educated in the art of decorum, they're able to move about with ease, even when confronted with stress? Etiquette is not to promote pride and arrogance, but rather grace and humility. I teach others how to encourage one another, promote family involvement, and teach others as well. This information is valuable for the entire household, community, staff, and industry.

My goal is to remove limits from your destiny. If I can get you to see it, then you will have the ability to seize it. Adopting basic manners and edifying another takes you to the head of your class.

There's nothing more beautiful than humility. Students of the school of life, but, more specifically, the school of etiquette, are lifelong students and teachers. They're continuously learning and growing, making those around them better. The end goal of every daughter must be to become a better, more exemplary student and teacher.

Every daughter must make the most of their positive characteristics. Make the most of them inside and out with proper grooming, clothing, self–worth and a positive influence on the lives surrounding you. Direction is needed. Life is better with a mentor who will point out where you can find the pitfalls as you travel the road of life.

Manners are lifetime skills that make "a world of difference" and the world a better place. Manners are life-skills that, if learned now, will be a comfortable practice for your future endeavors. Many people today know not the difference between an appetizer and dinner fork—although depending on your surroundings, that can be quite alright. But when you're thrust into the real world amongst the elite, you'd better have a clue. Manners can mean the difference between a promotion and a demotion. They are shown in your first impression of a firm handshake and a warm smile.

Some things hold true, no matter where you are. You can attend a picnic with friends or a formal dinner with your employees, and your basic good manners will shine through. You will be able to adapt to any environment of high estate and obtain favorable odds. The goal is to bring good decorum upfront.

LETTER 23
HEALTH CHECK

Dear Destiny,

I can only imagine how much further we could all be in life if we were all guaranteed mentors who corresponded with our life vision and goals. We would get to our destinations faster and get to a place where we could have the time to invent and create.

You most certainly need a healthy balance in a plethora of areas: physically, spiritually, emotionally, mentally and financially. There are so many aspects of physical health. I will break them down as we journey together.

I want to begin with you taking care of your body, so it can take care of you. Your health is your truest form of wealth. Without good health, all the money in the world doesn't matter. You must take good care of yourself with exercise and a balanced diet, so you'll have a better chance of living longer. Eating too much of anything is probably not good for you. Moderation is key. While eating healthy fruits, vegetables, and good starches and fats, you also need to drink water, water, *water*.

Drinking water and taking vitamins does so much for your body. First off, it keeps you alive and hydrated. You should drink warm water when you first get up in the morning. This helps with digestion and keeps you hydrated throughout the day. Here are a few benefits to drinking water: removal of waste, clear skin, good digestion, metabolism, blood circulation, and body temperature regulation. Along with drinking water, be sure to get a full night's rest. Talk to your physician about vitamins and which ones would be most beneficial to start a healthy journey early. Even taking daily multivitamin gummies or tablets can offer some of the daily nutrients your body needs.

Have you ever looked at a family and everyone seems to look just alike? DNA (Deoxyribonucleic Acid) is a self-replicating material that is found within almost all living organisms as the main constituent of chromosomes. It carries your genetic information. There are many things that an individual can be more susceptible to based upon their DNA. It makes you unique. Twins share the same DNA but can be identified by their fingerprints.

High blood pressure can run in a family's genes. Your risk for high blood pressure can increase based on your age, race or ethnicity. Blood pressure tends to rise as one ages. Families have similar lifestyles, behaviors, and environments that can play a role in their health. Health challenges like high blood pressure or diabetes are great indicators that you should try your best to live a healthy lifestyle to reduce your risk. Many families, especially within the same household, are more susceptible to duplicate health conditions because of similarities in diet, worrying and exercise – or the lack thereof. Listen to your body and make sure you attend your regularly scheduled checkups.

Just last year, I was minding my business when I woke up with lower abdominal pain. It felt like the worst cramp had come upon me. Mentally, I knew the pain was something more and I will tell you why. It took me until now to tell this story because it was so unbelievable. Every morning, I felt something on my side like a lump. It felt like something was standing up in my stomach. Yet seconds later, once I lifted my body from bed, it would be gone. Because there was no sign of the lump and because I slept alone, it was hard to describe what was happening without someone looking at me strangely.

One day, I headed to the gynecologist for my annual checkup. I braced myself and told the doctor what I was experiencing. She asked me if I was pregnant, and I answered that I've done nothing to get pregnant, so I certainly shouldn't be. She said she would check a few things to see if she felt something abnormal. She pressed firmly on my abdomen, asking me if I was experiencing pain, and I wasn't. The issue only took place every morning, but the proof was missing.

A year later, I returned to the gynecologist; however, it was a different person.

My new doctor was thorough. She ordered a pregnancy test, an MRI, and an ultrasound. She wanted to rule out what it wasn't, then she could see what it was. After careful testing, she found a fibroid so large that I had to undergo surgery. It was successfully removed, thanks to my incredible doctor. Dr. Lorie Johnson, an OB/GYN in Atlanta, Georgia, was my saving grace. She provided me with viable information and answered every question I posed. The fibroid was the size of a baby. After feeling uneasy for over a year, it was removed. I felt amazing afterward and my stomach was flat as a pancake.

Although I found that many women in my family had small fibroids, I was actually adding to it by not having a proper diet. I loved pickles, chips, and desserts, though now not as much. I placed my health above my desire and exercised discipline to cut back on eating unhealthy snacks. Now, I rarely eat them. Some things you *have* to do to stay in good health. The advantage of living a long, healthy life is a gift you can give to yourself. People may, however, be born with diseases or handicaps. Even with the best eating habits, it's still a fight to stay healthy.

Watch your sugar intake. A large consumption can cause weight gain, heart disease, diabetes, high blood pressure (caused by salt and sugar), cavities, poor sleep, mood problems and more. There are many great healthy recipes on the Internet to assist in making healthy food choices.

Take care of your health so you can do everything you dream of. Take the trip, buy the dog, purchase the investment property, and use the strength from your good health to take care of another. If I may reiterate, people who have all the money in the world would love to buy great health, but great health is priceless. You must work to keep it. You will end up getting *out* of your body what you've put *into* it.

LETTER 24
THE SPIRITUAL CONNECTION

Dear Destiny,

I've always wanted you to be a free thinker and to make your own decisions. If I raised you right, or to the best of my ability, everything I put in you will shine when the time comes.

We are spiritual beings with spiritual abilities. That inner voice is the voice that steers you to go straight, that redirects you when you get off the path and offers the option of peace over war and love over hate. The inner voice connects you with your reason for existence. It streamlines the connection of your bare feet to the earth, which confirms you have purpose here and assists you in trusting that your next breath will come, although you can't see it. It's the connection to a higher power who's responsible for creating a universe too complex to duplicate. A higher power who created a sun so beautiful that warms the earth, and yet, is too hot to approach. A moon that glows just enough to help us find our way but could only be accessed in its own timing. This Creator who watches over you also lives within you as a guide and a strength beyond your own abilities.

Everything that I've gone through has prepared me for something else or someone else. When I lost my brother, it weakened me so much so that other life trials paled in comparison. Setback is the best push because something keeps drawing you to the place of abundance. When I thought I would lose my job because our contract was ending, it caused me to start my own business. When people said I couldn't or wouldn't, I pressed past their voices, listened to my inner voice and persevered.

I speak of my past trials because I do believe having the ability to go through them and come out on the other side unscathed is a testament to my spiritual walk with God. When I was just four years old, I had a deep desire to know God more. I'm not sure where the desire came from or who introduced me to the fact that there was a God, but I knew that He held all the answers I needed since He was my creator. Always being inquisitive, I was okay with settling that there had to be a creator, one who orchestrated a human being who could walk, talk, blink, think, smile, cry and whose cells could reproduce themselves. I'm awed just thinking of it!

I wanted to learn more about God, so I went to church and opened myself up to an experience that revolutionized my life. Like everyone else, I endured trials and tribulations, setbacks and mishaps, but I knew my experience was different because I didn't walk the path alone. I chose to make Jesus my Savior because I felt rescued. Through the Word of God, I felt reassured and confirmed. My faith was the invisible rope I clung to and it kept pulling me forward.

I often see one person needing someone else to be for them the things I allow God to be in my life. He is consistent. One of the greatest lessons I ever learned was to manage my expectations, to know what I want from people and what I'm willing to give. We, as humans, need each other; however, we will constantly fail one another. It's just human nature. However, it's amazing that God never fails us because all things work out in the end with Him. This is the faith that I choose to have in Him, and I'm grateful for the lessons and blessings.

I do believe we all were created with spiritual yearning and that we all desire to be a part of something bigger than us. A comforter in the night, peace, wisdom to discern, faith in the impossible – that's who God is to me. He is joy amid sadness, and I'm so glad that He chose me.

My faith is so important because there have been times when I felt completely alone. I couldn't go off what things looked or felt like. My belief that God can and will do the impossible helped me understand that situations and circumstances would get better, and they always did.

"She is clothed
in strength and dignity,
and she laughs without
fear of the future.
— Proverbs 31:25 "

LETTER 25

EMOTIONS

Dear Destiny,

A student brought another young lady to me who was bawling her eyes out.

> Me: Why are you crying, is everything okay?
> (She could barely speak, but managed to get her words out)
> Student: He said I'm fat.
> Me: Okay, but why are you crying?
> Student: I'm fat and ugly.
> Me: Are you fat and ugly because he said it, or are you fat and ugly because that's how you see yourself?
> (She cried even more hysterically)
> Me: No one can define you and hurt you unless you give them permission to do so. Do you consider this person who called you these names a friend?
> Student: No, he's always talking crap about me, but it's true.
> (I gave it to her straight.)
> Me: Listen, I love you, but if you decide to cry every time a person says something about you, you will be crying for the rest of your life. The question is, *What are you saying about*

yourself and how do you see yourself? If you feel fat, there is something you can do about it; but you're more than your physical body. What about how smart you are, or how beautiful you are? You're allowing people to say what you believe you deserve, but there are two options: walk away, or tell that bully how you love every part of your body and you weren't created for his liking. *(I handed her a remote)*

Student: What's this?

Me: I'm handing you this remote control. I have a question for you. Who has the power to change the channel when it's in your hand?

Student: I do.

Me: Why?

Student: Because I've been given permission and the controller. Okay, I think I get it. Tell me more. *(She cracked a smile)*

Me: The person holding the remote has access and can make the decisions to turn you on or off, up or down. Who has the remote that's connected to your life?

Student: No one but me.

Me: That's hard to believe, seeing that you are in a frenzy because of words someone said about you who wanted to purposely hurt you. I believe the hurt comes because those are the words you've said or thought about yourself, and you allowed him to confirm them. Confirmation makes it more solid and that's where the hurt is derived. Let's work on you! Do you know what I see when I look at you?

Student: No, what, Ms. Willis?

Me: I see a beautiful, *exceptionally beautiful*, and intelligent young lady who will one day lead her generation. I see a strong, independent, courageous girl who can persevere over any obstacle that's placed in front of her.

Although you are sensitive, I see you using that to be all the more adamant about your passion in life – maybe teaching parents how to take care of their newborn babies or studying the shifting of tectonic plates warning communities of volcanic activity. I see a bright, successful agent of change and you, my child, have to look deeper until you see your true self. And when you do, what's within will begin to light the surface, and everyone else will see it as well.

How they decide to respond to you being fabulous is their business. Remain focused on your vision and goals. I see you and that's important; but what's *most important* is knowing that the person you're looking for who can change your life is right there in your mirror: *You.*

Who dictates your happiness? *You* are responsible for your happiness. It's not left up to anyone else; no one gets to control you unless you allow them to. You must be careful how much power you give someone to speak into your life, especially if they are not significant. This doesn't mean you won't have good days, bad days, lonely days, and sad days, but it does serve as a reminder that you get to choose.

LETTER 26
ATTITUDE

Dear Destiny,

There's nothing more important than your attitude. Let me explain with three different attitudes and the outcomes of each. According to Oxford Dictionary, an "attitude" is a settled way of thinking or feeling about someone or something, typically reflected in a person's behavior.

A. Based on your attitude toward life, are you all set on being the greatest person you can be, climbing the corporate ladder of leadership and success? Do you have an attitude of gratitude, knowing that you were born to be great, to make an impact in this world? Are ready to give your time, labor and direction to a world that has been awaiting your arrival? ....*type of attitude.*

B. Do you have an attitude of defeat, a "woe is me" attitude? Life has hit you with so many blows, it's just a matter of time and you will be knocked to the ground. Life isn't fair and darkness is more trustworthy than the light. You have the ability to use your mind and work with your hands, but dare you go out into this dangerous world and make it a better place? Life is a trap! ....*type of attitude.*

C. Do you have an attitude of entitlement? "I was here first, so you owe me." "There is no need to work for what belongs to me. I don't care that everyone else is in need and that they are willing to work; *I'm not.*" "If you're handing it out, I'm taking it—and I'm taking enough for me to eat today, tomorrow and in the days to come." ....*type of attitude.*

Attitude

Based on the *type of attitude* you have, it for sure will show in your body language.

Let's look at the results of these attitudes above.

A. Showing up ready to work with a smile on your face, greeting all those that come in your path, offering encouraging words and warm hugs, seeing where you're needed and being of service to all those that surround you—*type of attitude.*

B. Showing up unkempt, hair disheveled, and clothes wrinkled, wearing an expression that screams, "I don't want to be here!" You shake your head at any opportunity offered and you have no interest—*type of attitude.*

C. Nose flared, eyes rolling, cutting in line and daring anyone to step in before you. Physically snatching what doesn't belong to you and seeing nothing wrong with the behavior as a whole—*type of attitude.*

Everything starts with a thought. How are you thinking? How are you processing the things that pop into your mind? What are your surroundings like? What is the climate in the classroom, office or workstation? Do you feel there's a need to be guarded? Your attitude was once a thought and you either received that negative or positive thought, and it resulted in the attitude you then displayed.

If the attitude is negative and has already resulted in negative behavior, you're still safe. The first thing you need to do is look at your mind as a maze. Think about all the blocking forces that are keeping you from thinking positively. Avoid these forces, see your way out, and think your way out. Think and execute!

Three individuals come to mind when I think of having an attitude of a champion:

Simone Biles, Gabby Douglas, and Dominique Dawes ("Awesome Dawsome"), all-American gold medal gymnasts. They are some of the hardest working individuals in the world. Training is not just mental, but physical as well. All moves must be calculated. What's most rewarding is that the gymnasts see themselves as gold medalists even before they are awarded it. They choose to surround themselves with other winners.

These three women had positive attitudes before and after winning. They ignore the noise of those who say negative things and always present themselves as pleasant. Their attitude has to be determined before they get on the gym floor. There is so much they are up against, and yet they still must persevere. This is the mindset and attitude that must be adopted in order to outdo the competition.

No matter what's going on in your world, you have to know it will ultimately work out. "Mind over Matter" is important. Things can appear bleak, and you may fail many times; but when you finally cross the finish line and see your success, all of the struggles will finally seem worth it. You've developed an understanding of how to get from start to finish, and the muscles (strength) to prove it.

LETTER 27
FRIENDSHIP

Dear Destiny,

Have you ever told a lie and it was too late to pull it back? Have you ever told a lie that destroyed a relationship of your own or others without that being your intention? Lies separate, destroy, and kill; they are unhealthy and show a lack of integrity and good character.

Once an individual finds out you lied, they may forgive you; but sometimes earning back their trust can take some time. For some, it can never be earned again. When a person becomes vulnerable enough to share their truth with you, don't carry it back to others and put your own twist on it. Steer clear of drama, gossip and slandering someone's character. Choose your friends wisely and be honest. You only have your word – be a woman of your word! Honesty is the best policy!

Not all of your friends have to be the same. In fact, it's healthy to have friendships where each individual can be unique in their own way. If you have to suffocate your friend, pointing them in every direction they must go, it may be a little taxing for you.

Friends don't let friends go down the wrong path. If you have a friend who has made a non-negotiable (a promise to themselves) that she won't drink, and she decides to go out with other friends to party and drink for the occasion, it's cool to remind her of her non-negotiable. That will be a tough call if the results of her drinking lead her to drunkenness and you have to step in. First, make sure you're safe and that someone you trust knows what's going on. Decide and trust that all things will work out for the good.

All friendships have their ups and downs, and loyalty is a mark of a true friend. Know those who labor among you for certain. Some friends you can talk to about almost everything and your stories are safe—even if you two fall out and never talk again. You check this "loyalty meter" based upon this person talking about others. The people who never have negative things to say about others are great picks when it comes to venting. But, remember the rule of thumb: never tell anyone anything that you can't bear to hear repeated.

Some friends you just can't talk to about almost anything, but are there rather for, say, their fashion sense. You can't turn the shopping friend into the friend you vent to. You have to keep what you value with each friend separately. This friend can't hold water, but you know this because they tell *everyone's* business, including their own, along with the things they promised not to say. They don't only tell you, but to anyone who will listen. They're always inviting themselves into conversations even when they haven't been welcomed in.

You're your sister's keeper if you come with your sister. Leave with her unless there's no way you can get her out of deep trouble without putting yourself into harm's way. If you find yourself in a compromising, unsafe situation, contact someone immediately. Always steer clear of putting yourself or others in harmful situations.

How to Apologize

"I'm sorry" or "forgive me" are only introductions to an apology. Apologies must come with sincerity. The proper way to apologize is to talk through a matter and allow both sides to be heard. There's a lot that can be gained from the discussion. However, sometimes it's safe to just walk away and leave the relationship behind you. It's always good to remain cordial and not hold any hate or malice within your heart because unfortunately, the other person typically gets to go free and your mind is now bound, replaying a story over and over again.

How to be friendly without being a creep?

Be friendly, be kind, and be authentic. Don't let people walk over you. Say, "Yes," when you want to, and say, "No," when you desire.

What If *You're* the Friend that Others Desire to "Let Go"?

Find out why people don't desire to be in your company. If everyone has the same exact negative things to say about you, this may be a great opportunity to embrace beneficial change into your life. If everyone feels you're unpleasant to be around and you're okay with that, then continue as you are, but you'll get the same results. If you really wish to change, "own your stuff."

Admit when you are wrong and apologize, if you can. It takes maturity to find out if you've wronged someone, and by then, you may be on separate sides of the globe. The only person you can change is *you*. It's easier to sleep when you know you've done right by others.

Check Your Bitterness

Are you bitter about something? Is there someone you haven't forgiven? Do you hate the way someone treated you growing up and you are giving out that same exact energy? Ask yourself the hard questions and give yourself the honest answers. If you're suffering from a broken past, know that professional help may be an option to put your life back on track. You don't have to live broken. People deserve to get to know the amazing you. You deserve to have an amazing life with *amazing you!*

LETTER 28
IT'S A GIRL THING!

Dear Destiny,

Ouch, Ouch, Ouch! You don't get to choose the day, time, moment or event, when a cramp (dysmenorrhea) comes unexpectedly. They often come to kick butt. Let's talk menstrual cycle.

It still shocks me how vocal young girls are concerning their menstrual cycle. Growing up, it was a conversation only heard in health class or amongst your closest friends. Nowadays, conversations happen amid boys and girls alike, and young ladies will quickly say why they must sit out on activities due to their period. Periods are no secret because almost every female in the world, at some point, should have one. There's no need for the subject to be taboo. However, the changes you experience in your body should be private if you desire because it's your personal business.

Every female's body is different and so, their cycles may slightly differ. Some bleed very heavily, while others are light. Some have excruciating cramps, while others breeze by with limited pain. There is a plethora of treatments for the pain endured during the menstrual cycle. They include, but are not limited to aspirin, naproxen (Aleve), ibuprofen (Advil), and many other over-the-counter (OTC) pain medications, all of which you should consult your physician or your parents, if you're a minor, before taking. There are other options and holistic approaches to take for relief. Even a good nap can help the pain to subside. The body is changing from a child's body into an adult body and is now capable of reproduction or giving birth. The cycle happens monthly and there are signs to let you know the period is about to arrive.

Mood swings, anyone? About a week before your period starts, you may notice some signs of it being "that time of month," along with emotional changes. As we talked about before, you must manage your emotions. When you're mentally and emotionally irritated, you've got to pull it all back together. These physical and emotional symptoms are known as premenstrual syndrome (PMS), and they can make or break you if you let them. For example, one may experience fatigue, headaches, food cravings, and a not-so-kind attitude a couple weeks prior to bleeding. Then the week before, it can be mood swings, anger, anxiety, stress and lack of patience, straight into the period which could be packaged with bloating, and low abdominal pain and tenderness of breasts.

I would get so emotional prior to my cycle that I would want to save the koala bears in Australia and help everyone realize how much I loved them. And, yes, this was my daily behavior mixed with being extremely emotional. There are other ways to balance PMS. First, be conscious of the time of the month. You should keep track using either a calendar or by downloading an app to keep you aware. Try journaling, a massage, exercising, sleep and/or meditation to gather yourself.

What exactly is a *period*? The average female will have their first period between the ages of eleven and fourteen. A menstrual period occurs when a woman discharges through the vagina, producing blood and other materials from the lining of the uterus monthly.

The female body prepares itself for a possible pregnancy each month. A thicker lining is developed in the uterus, and a mature egg is released from the ovaries, which in turn can be fertilized by sperm. If the egg that was released isn't fertilized, pregnancy won't occur during that cycle. The built-up uterine lining that was developed is now shed by the body.

Most females use a sanitary pad or tampon during bleeding; there are natural menstrual products that are now available for purchase. The typical time one should change their sanitary pad is approximately every four hours and a tampon every two hours. These times can vary a bit based on the flow. No one wants to develop TSS (toxic shock syndrome), or toxins produced by bacteria. Always read the instructions that come with the products you use to ensure safety. It's important to change your feminine hygiene products at the appropriate time and bathe during your cycle so there's no odor and to prevent overflow.

How long will it last? Once your menstrual cycle starts, you're locked in until menopause, which typically happens between the ages of forty-five and fifty-five. The bleeding lasts for three to five days and could be longer for some except during pregnancy, when the menstrual cycle ceases. If you experience bleeding for longer than seven days, you should see your gynecologist to make sure everything is working properly.

Because PMS could put you on a rollercoaster of moods, it's safe to say you need to know your non-negotiables prior to making any decisions during these times. You may experience feelings you've never known your body could desire, and you may want to eat every piece of chocolate in a one-mile span, *but you should not give in.*

Non-negotiables are things you answer yes or no to prior to being tempted with the question. When someone poses the question, it can't be negotiated. The answer is solely *no.* I learned of non-negotiables at the age of 11. I made the decision that sexual intercourse could and should wait until marriage. I weighed the pros and cons, and keeping my body being disease-free and my relationships healthy was something I truly desired. I thought that when I'm good enough to a particular man that he chooses to marry me, and vice versa, that's when we should come together as one and consummate the marriage. Many decisions are made when an individual is emotional, so non-negotiables are safe "go-to's", so your emotions don't answer for you.

As you mature you will continue to learn more about your body, your likes and dislikes. Having a menstrual cycle is a beautiful thing when you have a clear understanding of how the body is created to function, heal and cleanse itself.

It helps mentally to look at it as a blessing rather than a curse, and to know you are fully equipped to understand your moods and emotions and be in complete control.

"

We delight in the
beauty of the
butterfly, but rarely
admit the changes it
has gone through to
achieve that beauty.
-Dr. Maya Angelou

"

LETTER 29
TECH ETIQUETTE:
THE AGE OF SOCIAL MEDIA

Dear Destiny,

Digital etiquette, or *netiquette* as it is sometimes called, is a basic set of rules you should follow to make the Internet a better place for yourself and for others. Just as there are rules of etiquette in real life, as in face-to-face encounters, there are also rules you should follow while online. Most importantly, we must remember that the "digital" world is not all that different from the "real" world with respect to proper etiquette. They are one and the same.

Once you join the social media world, you are forever a part of it. You now have a digital footprint, which tracks your steps from one website to another—even from one form of social media to another.

If you don't want people in your personal business, don't post it. You shouldn't be upset when people comment on what you've posted or share their opinion. If the person is not attacking you or being negative, unfortunately they are free to speak. People have the ability to go further than a comment because they can like, dislike, or even share your post, giving other people permission to know about and share in your business.

When you post anything on social media, you must decide that you don't mind hearing it again. One of the greatest pieces of wisdom I've garnered from my teacher, Dr. Dedria Willis, is when she looked me square in the eyes and said, "Never tell anyone anything that you don't want repeated." Trust yourself with your secrets. Never post inappropriate material, nasty messages, or nude pictures or videos. Do not post anything that could incriminate you, especially when you're trying to get a job in the future or becoming a boss yourself. You may not only find your page in social media jail, but you also can't take back what you've put out there.

Don't entertain a bully in your online space; rather, disconnect immediately. Pertaining to negativity, your online presence is equal to your physical presence. You deserve a healthy digital space. Written words can be worse than those spoken; they not only carry a heavy negative weight, but they are forever available to go back to and can never leave the digital world. Block people, when necessary, to protect your own sanity. Also, if you see anything strange, tell someone in charge. You can save a life or lives by reporting inappropriate behavior, threats and self-harm messages or videos.

When it comes to communicating with a good friend or acquaintance online, it may be better to reach out to that person and have a live conversation. Relationships are not worth losing over misunderstandings. It's often difficult to discern a person's true intent with typed words and without knowing the correct context or tone of voice the message was delivered in. Steer away from heated arguments and profane talk on the Net and in text. Avoid language that may come across as strong or offensive. Remember, typing in all caps can easily be considered yelling.

Rule #1 The Golden Rule: Treat others as you want to be treated. Don't immediately reply. If something deserves your attention, talk it over with someone wise who can help you make the best decision. If you have to think awfully hard about it, you probably shouldn't respond.

If it's negative, let the thought pass and don't type it. Just keep it to yourself and eliminate it from your thoughts. Be conscious of the effect your comments on social media have on others, both short and long-term. Ask yourself questions like: Does this person battle with low self-esteem and am I making light of their struggle?

Always make sure your content is appropriate and that it represents your brand and the person you are. We never see or hear of brands like McDonald's, Chick-fil-A, or Whole Foods getting into heated debates online, and that's because they have an image to uphold—*and so do you.*

Taking Phone Calls

Technology can be abused, misused and addictive. Set aside a time for technology and try not to let it intrude on family time. Give people your undivided attention. Don't text and talk when the conversation is serious and deserves your full attention. Depending on where you're dining, check to see if you should have your phone on your person during the dining experience. Does the host have their phone out? Also, give the road your undivided attention while driving. Never text and drive; your life matters, as well as those who are on the road along with you.

Make sure you say exactly what you mean. There are many types of code words used and you don't want to get caught up in anything. It's important to know the language of the Internet.

Don't leave any room to be caught up in anything negative. More often than not, people have had text messages read in a court of law that resulted in charges ranging from a minor infraction to felony.

If you have friends who are not on social media, there may be a good reason. Consider their privacy and ask permission to post information, pictures and screenshots. Always review a text before you send it. I've mistakenly texted all types of things unintentionally just because I didn't double check.

Take social media breaks so you can stay in tune with people and the things you have going on around you. I trust that you will do extremely well. You're talented, brave, and strong. Use your skills of wisdom to defy the odds and make your platform educable and profitable. Time and energy are money!

LETTER 30
FINANCIAL WISDOM

Dear Destiny,

The conversation we've all been waiting for: "Show me the money."

We all have the ability to be business owners and create or duplicate a product or service that will help simplify people's lives. The best way to figure out what you can sell is to look at the needs of others. What are some things people need every day, like toothpaste, socks and hairbrushes? Figure out how to get them to choose your product over what they've been using possibly all their lives. Starting a business is not hard, but you must have a plan in store before you begin. Follow the trends and observe your demographics' buying patterns. The plan keeps you on track. It helps you gauge how you're spending your time and energy, and your assets versus liabilities. That way, you can find out if it's worth it.

Take one idea and come up with a product or service you would like to provide. Study that product or service and see how profitable it will be. After discovering that this product is a great choice to find your target customer, see what their needs are and if they are willing to purchase from you. You must know where you will find your customer—whether on social media or at a local monthly meeting. Who is your competition, and how can you better service the customer so that they choose *you*?

You don't have to start big, but the only way to succeed is to *start*. You must execute! You must have a color scheme. What colors attract people to your product or service? Let's say your product is bubble gum. What colors come to mind when people think of the item? Create a logo and use those colors! Think about the strengths and weaknesses of your business and describe the problem that you will solve with your product or service.

Although you may start small, you can finish with a phenomenally successful business. When you write the vision for your business, you'll determine if you are looking to be in a brick-and-mortar (building). How many employees will you have working for you and how much will you pay each?

It's important to save and invest. Always have resources saved for a rainy day. Know what you can afford and the risk you are taking. It's okay to take a risk; just calculate the losses and gains ahead of time. Once you get your business down to a science, you can start applying for credit and purchase more products while holding your money in the bank and building your credit portfolio. When your business really starts doing well after you have registered and incorporated it, you may have to ask for some help; but there are many resources online.

You will learn problem-solving strategies and so much more from starting a business. You will definitely be tested, and your goal has to be met to provide customer satisfaction.

Continue to have a great attitude doing business with every customer you meet and be ethical in every dealing. Money can't buy morality; it takes self-respect to guide our ethical dealings, making for long term relationships.

I already see your vision coming to pass.

Here's a small piece of your Vision Board. Fill out the form below. You can refer back to this "dream starter" and begin to watch things manifest. The universe will assist you in helping all your dreams come to pass.

My Business Plan

For Creatives

Executive Summary

Include your purpose, mission,
and vision for your business.

Market Analysis

Include the customers your'e targeting,
your competitors and your plan of success.
What are your strengths, weaknesses,
opportunties and threats?
Where will you position your business
in the market to attract customers.

Operations

Include the logistics from raw materials to
getting product or service to the end consumer.
How much money to start and run your business,
how much of a profit will you receive?

Long Term Goals

Include equipment investments and/or
expansion, or a new location, what are your
long-term goals, where do you see yourself?

Human Resources

Include all indiviuals needed to run your
successful business, how many, how much are
you paying them, what experience or
skillset is needed and who will train them.

Financial Plan

Include the steps to becoming a profitable business.
Research and include an income statement,
balance sheet and cash-flow statement.

www.ShamaliaWillis.com

LETTER 31

FREEDOM TO CHOOSE

Dear Destiny,

You must be conscious of the many battles that people face on a daily basis. We all have to be sensitive to what others are experiencing and suffering from. You don't have to be a victim to sympathize with people and acknowledge that we all should be treated fairly, no matter the color of our skin or the content of our character. You don't have to join every movement, but you should respect the voices of those fighting for freedom and equal rights.

Peer pressure is real, and it happens every day. Remember when we talked about those non-negotiables and how we have to make decisions that are best for us before leaving home? When peer pressure comes about you will have to lean on those decisions and not wrestle with whether you should or if you shouldn't give in.

When I was in middle school, "the land of peer pressure," students seemed to be doing a little bit of everything. Some used profanity, smoked, drank alcohol and some were even sexually active. When I talked to those who were taking part in these activities, they would try to convince me that everybody was doing it. This is where the good lessons I was taught kicked in. Internally,

I would think, *First off, everybody can't be doing it if I'm not taking part; and secondly, I'm not everybody.*

The thing with hitting adolescence is that you understand there's a world within a world. Mistakes will be made, but they are learning tools to help you navigate back to the right path. This is why, when I speak of integrity, I emphasize being consistently you. Shutting out wisdom and joining your peers' movements can be extremely dangerous and can happen at any age. If it's something you will be ashamed to talk about in the light, don't do it in the dark because these things always come to the surface.

When people know better, I really believe they *do* better. That's why it's my job to teach you what you should know. Many of my friends in school tried things at the tender age of twelve. There are things you may know, but as I said before, at that age you have a limited picture. You have blocking agents that prevent you from seeing what you *need* to see, and that can have the greatest effect on you.

Diseases are real! I remember being in class and seeing these graphic pictures of individuals who had herpes, syphilis, and other sexually transmitted diseases (STDs). Looking at the individuals' faces, you would never know they were infected. When studies say that four out of five people (that's 80%) in a community has a certain disease, you can't be locked in with the notion that it can't happen to you, especially if you're sexually active at a young age. There are people who battle with treating themselves for diseases they didn't bring on themselves and yet it's now a part of their lives. You only get one body, so you have to take care of it.

Daughter, make wise decisions. If things don't look safe, avoid them. At a young age, never travel alone; as an adult, someone should always know where you are and where you're expected to be for safety reasons. No one should touch you in a manner in which you don't wish to be touched. There's nothing you can do to deserve being fondled or raped. A *no* is a *no*!

There is nothing you can do to deserve being touched inappropriately. There's no outfit you can wear, and no shorts are too short. If you see someone making advances and you don't feel comfortable, speak up. Friends don't always protect you, so you have to protect yourself. Watch the crowds you choose to hang around. If someone touches you in an inappropriate manner, tell someone in authority. For so long, women have fought for their voices to be heard. Even after that, it took some time for women to gain the tenacity to tell their stories.

I had no clue how many people were victims of rape and abuse, until I was an adult. What's even worse is that just as many people were not believed when the evidence was clear, when women have been victimized and those closest to them didn't believe them. For some, it took them into silence; others lived with hate in their heart toward those who didn't believe them. I do understand, however, that those who profess false stories make it bad for those whose stories are true. I'm so glad so many men and women have gained the power to tell their stories.

And for those who remain silent, locking up inside the very thing that took your voice, I see you, and I pray for you. I hope you will find the strength to release your voice, to break free and be healed. You're beautiful, and you deserve your freedom. Heal so you can be healthy enough to find your place in this world and assist the next person on their journey to healing.

LETTER 32
LIFE AND DEATH ARE IN THE POWER OF THE TONGUE

"Politeness is the art of choosing among your thoughts."
– Madame de Stael

Dear Destiny,

You do have the right to "let it go" in your own time, but is it worth missing your destiny? What did they say about you? How many times did you give them a pass until you were plain sick and tired of being walked all over? Did you allow them to control you and did they say it enough times that you started believing what they said about you? In your mind are you fighting why they talked about you or are you fighting the words spoken that you now embrace as truth?

Words have been given to us all and they are a gift. Words can be strung together to create some of the most beautiful ballads, or they can offer to a bride or groom the assurance they need as to why they chose their mates as they speak their vows aloud. Words hold enough power to cheer an amputee Olympian to the finish line and place first. And yet, negative words can paralyze a child who otherwise could actually walk, like in the Lifetime movie, *Love You to Death,* or defeat a now-former NBA player who suffered a knee injury, but had so much life left within him.

People speak negative and positive words into the atmosphere every day. You are responsible for the words you speak and listen to. Who are you listening to? As you listen to the words that fall upon the soil of your mind, you must filter them. Let the good come in and question the bad. "Do these words belong?" After that, toss out the bad because letting the thoughts stay long enough to take root causes you to lock them in as a possible truth. It can also choke the good that you've recently let in.

Words are small seeds, and your mind is a garden. The representation of the words you've received is depicted by the plants that have grown and bloomed in your garden. Water your garden by speaking great things over yourself and cultivate those blooms by sifting out the bad.

What people say behind your back can be damaging, but you're not obligated to chase around what is not true. Fix the story, if given the opportunity, but know that the truth always seems to find itself paying a visit to the person who seeks after it.

Choose words that will uplift and encourage, words that will cause someone who is down and out to see a light of hope. Physical therapists choose their words wisely. They see the potential within their patients, and they say things like, "You can do it," or "One more step," or "You're almost there." We need these people in our corners, our circles, our small groups – in our lives. They're encouragers! The best thing about encouragers is that their lives may not be working out the way they desire, yet they are selfless and conjure up enough strength to help someone else make it through another day.

In all my years of teaching, one of the greatest rewards is speaking life into my students based on what they desire to be. I had a student by the name of Ga'Nylah Ross. Ga'Nylah desires to be a lawyer, so every time I see her, I refer to her as such. How I see my students is particularly important. It gives me the ability to expect more out of them based on where they desire to be in the future, and to also give them a measuring stick so when I'm not around, they still know what's expected of them. They can perceive reality differently! How we see people does not have to line up with a "right-now" type of situation; it could have everything to do with building their faith for where they're going.

There's no timeframe as to how early we should begin speaking over children. There are many studies that show parents speaking over the child within their womb. My good friends, Melissa and Tayon Shelby, gave birth to two beautiful children. Since the births of Sony and Ivy, a few of us refer to them as "Dr. Sonny" and "Dr. Ivy." We are locked into the fact that they will become something exceptional. They'll be the future leaders and will make a great impact in our country.

Anger, as we talked about before, is a strong emotion that must be handled correctly. The problem is not becoming angry, but rather *staying* angry. Staying angry and allowing it to lead to resentment could often hurt you. It can increase anxiety, blood pressure, and lead to other health risks. When someone has wronged you or even caused grave danger, you must find a way to deal with it so that you don't allow that person or situation to remove the light and life inside yourself. You can't give your life away – you're needed.

Have you ever heard the quote, "Resentment is like swallowing poison and expecting the other person to die?" You are responsible for the energy you carry. Wishing evil on another won't heal you. Take the time and heal yourself so that the situation won't get the best of you. You must forgive. Forgiveness is releasing an individual from the wrong they've done to you so that you can either restore the relationship or continue living life. We forgive because we ourselves are not perfect and may unintentionally hurt another. We want to be extended that same forgiveness.

Watch the seeds people try to plant about others. It's important to hear the wisdom of those you respect and admire, but it's important to give people a fair chance. Someone may call someone you don't even know a liar, and yet a seed has been planted. This information can sway your opinion, influence or lead you to treat this individual differently. How would you like it if someone told someone else information about you that wasn't true? Words cause you to prematurely judge an individual without getting to know the person for yourself. Getting to know them and allowing the person to prove the spoken information wrong helps eliminate what was spoken about them over time. However, if a trusted individual gave you that kind of information, do tread lightly in the area of conversation until the person proves otherwise.

Words have power, so choose yours wisely. The words you choose to speak of another should always be in respect and so much in line with the truth that, if that person was sitting there, they wouldn't be able to hear anything false. If thoughts precede words, we should probably work on our thinking.

"Summing it all up, friends, I'd say you'll do best by filling your minds and meditating on things true, noble, reputable, authentic, compelling, gracious—the best, not the worst; the beautiful, not the ugly; things to praise, not things to curse." (Philippians 4:8, MSG)

Meditation is helpful to keep your thoughts under control. Choosing what you let into your mental space is important. You're responsible for your thoughts, so think positively so that the words that come from your mouth will also be positive and you will receive the same in return.

"Politeness is the art of choosing among your thoughts."

-Madame de Stael ♥

LETTER 33

TRIUMPH

Dear Destiny,

Think about the home you live in or maybe the school you attend. They all began with a thought that was carried out to produce a result. Perhaps the thought was to build an educational facility where students can participate in hands-on learning or maybe the thought was to build a house that a loving family could call home. First the thought, then the will to do it came. Then, the execution came. But what do you do when unexpected situations occur?

Picture this: The builder started with one brick and laid beside it another and another until that row was complete. After scaling halfway up the foundation, the diligent builder stepped back to see that he was making great progress. A storm came and half the structure was knocked down to the ground. Ultimately, the builder discovered his foundation was not solid. The only way the building would be completed is to simply start again.

This is where you can separate the finisher from the one who throws in the towel. The builder has every good excuse to quit because, as you know, he was building diligently. Listen beautiful, throwing in the towel can't be an option in this life. You must finish what you started. Make the decision to begin again and focus.

We must tackle life like the builder, one brick (step) at a time. The end goal may seem far away, whether it be graduating school, saving for your first car, or becoming the best version of yourself. You must put one foot in front of the other and finish what you started. When life happens, think through the options. Cry if you need to, but get back in the game.

Let's talk about a few obstacles that life can throw your way and how to recover from them or learn to live your best life along with the outcome. Here are a few tools for unexpected adversity. But first, make a conscious decision to live and get your life on a positive path.

Teen Mom

We've talked clearly about prevention, but we haven't talked about how to bounce back if you've had a baby in your teenage years. This is indeed a life-altering experience. You are now responsible for yourself, as well as your child. But life goes on and the days get better. I sat down with a teen mom who gave me some tools to make the best out of the difficult situation.

- Your child is your first priority.
- Build a community for your child of safe individuals, parents, teachers, leaders, mentors and role-models.
- Take time to relax and take mental breaks.
- Get outside, take walks with your child and breathe fresh air.
- Set a vision in place to not let time get away from you.
- Live alongside the goals you set for your child, while your child is in daycare, work. When your village is available

take weekend classes, use your youth (energy) to your advantage.

Just don't give up on your dreams. Tweak them to accommodate your child.

Loss

Some things change you momentarily and others are life-altering. I sat down with Ky'Ann to talk with her about bouncing back after losing her mother at the age of fifteen.

What are the hardest challenges you have trying to move on without your mom?
Her not showing up for events and being there when I really need her.

How do you live with those challenges?
I think about the support she would give me and the words she would say if she was present and find peace in that.

How do u keep her memory alive?
Pictures, memories and working hard to make her proud.

What are the daily strategies to not fall into depression?
Knowing that she wouldn't want me to live my life sad. So I push to show up and, even if I have moments, I gather myself and not use it as an excuse. I take it one day at a time.

Depression
According to the American Psychiatric Association, depression (major depressive disorder) is a common and serious medical illness that negatively affects how you feel, the way you think, and how you act. Some signs of depression are difficulty concentrating, thoughts of death or suicide, or feeling worthless or guilty, just to name a few. Depression causes feelings of sadness and/or a loss of interest in activities you once enjoyed. It can lead to a variety of emotional and physical problems and can decrease your ability to function at work and at home. Fortunately, depression is also treatable.

If you feel you are suffering from depression, reach out to an adult who can assist you in getting an appointment to get the proper help and/or diagnosis. Go through mental checks with someone you trust and let them know when you're not doing well. If you hear negative voices that are fighting against doing good, you must not take heed to the voice. If you feel yourself getting down often, develop a plan.

- Use a journal to keep track of your emotions
- Try to track what causes the downward spirals
- Know the difference between depression and anxiety and have a "go-to" solution for each.
- Anxiety is when you feel uneased or have a feeling of worry and you can't always control the outcome.
- Go against your emotions if they lead you to doing things that are harmful or dangerous. Exchange those negative emotions with positive responses
- Keep this plan close

Lack

Wealth is found in knowledge coupled with the will to do.

You can get up from any situation you find yourself in. It doesn't matter the stigma that was once placed on you from those near or far. Work in your time and build one brick at a time. I often hear people talk about growing up in lack "back in the days." They didn't have all they desired to eat, to wear, to enjoy. The greatest benefit for them as they matured was the knowledge to change their situation. The knowledge came from information, books and listening to those who had wisdom. Although there was lack, there was still a thirst for life and for travel. Often, that interest came from listening, watching or reading another's life by an author some thousands of miles away.

If you started in a place of lack, remember you can shape your outcome on the side of success. You may not be able to change your current situation, but you can adjust your sails to float your boat toward the best coast where you can make a new life for yourself and perhaps others in the near future. Lack doesn't have to be forever. Prepare for the life that you want to live and prepare for the fresh air you desire to breathe. Help at the local grocery store or help with yard work in the community. Take a moment one day soon and read Robert Kyaosaki's book, Rich Dad Poor Dad.

Intellect is afforded to those who seize it. You can think yourself out of any situation. It may take some time, but keep working at it. You will end with an amazing work ethic and the ability to change bleak situations into amazing outcomes. You will over come adversity. You will get to the place you desire. Just decide, get up, and finish.

You got this! Triumph!

PASSION & PERSEVERANCE

I have nothing in common with lazy people who blame others for their lack of success. Great things come from hard work and perseverance. No excuses.

– Kobe Bryant

Dear Destiny,

Sometimes, it's so difficult to be strong when you are in a battle in life. You find yourself pushing, but it feels like life is pushing back toward you. What do you do when it feels like life has you pinned down and you can barely breathe? You have to take a deep breath and push back through circumstances and situations.

The fight doesn't stop; but with experience from your past battles, you gain strategy and strength for the next round. You're fully equipped with the wisdom to handle anything that comes toward you. We all have different strategies for how we deal with pain, loss, and disheartening situations, but you have to find what works for you – especially when giving up *is not an option*.

For me, when life gets difficult, the first thing I do is strategize and prioritize. I keep moving on rough terrain and keep swimming when the water becomes turbulent. I keep moving forward, and that alone is fighting back. My strategy is to understand what I'm facing and find a way out which doesn't always come immediately.

I prioritize by understanding what I can do now. If I stop swimming, I will drown; but if I keep going, I will surface to at least catch another breath. Life can sometimes feel like an invisible hand pushing us back; but if we persevere, we will make it.

This has not always been the case. I used to be so set on being non-confrontational, that I would give up any opportunity that came my way if the environment wasn't conducive for my mind to be at rest. I also know the timing has always been right for me. If you're not ready to battle something internal, wait until you can mentally handle the repercussions. This time I was ready – not for the other person, but for me. I needed to prove to myself that I could have a healthy confrontation and will be alright in the end, no matter the outcome.

For the first time in my life, someone called me with an issue that somehow, I became a part of. Instead of holding back, I garnered the strength to speak my truth and let the chips fall where they would. It was the most liberating experience to date. I didn't care if they agreed with me or not; I took the opportunity to say what I was thinking. I was tactful and I was still careful about being polite. I pulled myself up and exited that conversation, and I never felt so liberated. I spoke my truth and left it there. From there, all parties had to choose a new path. That's just a part of life.

When I think about an individual who encompasses perseverance, the one person who quickly comes to mind is Mr. Tyler Perry. Mr. Perry defied the odds and carved out his own path. He didn't make excuses when life got hard. He was one who displayed hard work, grace, humility, honesty and dedication. To date, Mr. Perry has produced, written, and directed his very own stage plays, television shows, and movies. Mr. Perry has told stories about being poor and being raised by a single parent. He slept in his car. He rented out a large theatre, and not many showed up; but he didn't let his fight to achieve his dreams stop him.

Take note from those who let nothing stop them. Take note from Devon and Semaj Willis who are both passionate about technology. Take note from the "Kobe Bryants" of the world, the "President Barack Obamas" and the "Celine Dions." You have everything in you to push the limits and change the world. When we see the word *passion,* we can look a little closer and see "Pass-I-On." How do you want people to remember you? With what will your name be associated?

Tyler Perry	Tyler Perry Studios
Shirley Chisolm	First Black Congresswoman
Sha'Malia Willis	International Educator
_____	_____
Place Your Name Here	How you would like to live and be remembered

LETTER 35

THE ABSENT PARENT

Dear Destiny,

Growing up, we always told the story about Alvester having to ask his dad if he could go to the store with everyone. It was a great, fall day, and all the kids were on the block, enjoying one another's company. In between bike riding, we would take a break on the first available porch. Shortly after, someone came up with the bright idea of going to the store, which was about six houses down. As we proceeded to shift gears, grab our bikes and go to the store, Alvester said, "Hold up one second, I gotta tell my dad."

Everyone looked stunned.

"You have a father in the house?" My sister shouted. Everyone erupted in laughter. Although everyone knew Alvester had a father who was present in his life, it was still a shock because so many fathers were missing on a daily basis in the community. Even if they were there part-time, children rarely had to run things by their fathers. There were many single mothers left with taking care of children, cooking, cleaning, going to work, and being real-life superheroes. Here's the shocker: the fathers were originally present, but something happened in the mid-90s where the rate of single-parent homes just skyrocketed. The absence of fathers was not only felt amongst the children, but for some of us, it was clear in our behavior.

What we go through becomes a part of our makeup. Oftentimes, it is the reason we respond the way we do. Growing up, there were many fathers absent in various households and the mother was the sole provider. Often, these fathers came around whenever convenient for them. There were other times when children would wait on their fathers who promised yet again to pick them up so they could spend some time together. When the father breaks his promise and never shows up, the child is left feeling alone, abandoned, and deceived.

There are different things that can happen to the child that affects their future. The child:

- loses trust;
- is unable to form healthy relationships;
- begins to blame themselves for their parent's absence;
- is emotionally traumatized.

The child moves into adulthood and continues to trust, but when a promise is broken, it causes:

- Depression and withdrawal
- Anxiety and flashbacks
- Resentment towards all
- Toxic relationships

The presence of another father figure can be painful as well. Even in the next generation, the baggage they carry begins to affect everyone around them as adults. They may even find it difficult to parent their own child(ren) because there was no model for them to observe pertaining to parent-child relationships.

From childhood to adulthood, so many carry the feeling of "I'm not lovable." They begin to search for love, and every time they turn up empty-handed, their relationships end in chaos. Not only was their childhood hard and lonely, but their adulthood as well. This is not the only factor that individuals carry over into adulthood when they are mistreated as children. They are also affected by addictions, trauma, molestation, poverty, and the like. But there is a way *out*!

If you could understand how certain traumas led you to certain decisions, you can fix the little girl inside you, you can forgive yourself, and this will automatically begin to restore the "grown woman" so you can be the fierce powerhouse you were born to be!

First, you have to own your emotions and understand where they stem from. You have to admit that it has burdened you. Start to work on healing the wounds instead of just putting a bandage over it and not speaking about it. You must fight against the bad thoughts with good thoughts and daily affirmations. Repeat those affirmations until you believe them. Even when thoughts of jealousy arise, you must embrace being happy for others in spite of your inner emotions. Affirmations always find themselves as part of your daily routine and at some point, you empower yourself with the very words that will bring you life. Try speaking the words below to set the tone for a greater life.

AFFIRMATIONS

- I will no longer replay the negative effects of my past when I feel them coming up.
- I will instead think of how grateful I am to be freed from the chains of yesterday.
- I have love in my heart toward all and no jealousy or envy is found within me.
- All those who are currently in my life are here for mutually beneficial reasons.
- I am grateful for my current and future relationships.
- I will no longer be a victim of my past hurts.
- I am responsible for myself.
- I am loving and am loved.
- I celebrate the new me.
- I am complete.
- I am whole.
- I am free.

LETTER 36
FOCUS & SOLITUDE

Dear Destiny,

This is a great time to stay focused and work on where you see yourself in the future. Oftentimes, when you get really focused, everything that can and will distract you comes knocking at your door. Don't get up from your place of planning to answer. It takes discipline and perseverance to work on your life and help others.

We've come so far from where we once were. We've covered so much ground and we've reached a place of forgiveness, restoration, and are now finding our happy place. We are releasing ourselves of soul ties – those relationships that are neither healthy nor beneficial, but they are indeed comfortable. We tell ourselves that we deserve better and we need better. Where we are going, there is no room for mediocrity. Through discipline, passion and cleansing, we are shaping our lives for our future desires.

You must beware of unhealthy ties and ask yourself, "What's in you that's attracting you to them/it?" Sometimes, we can have ties with people we know mean us no good, but again are a great comfort. You have to let timewasters and cushions go so you can put the healthy people in that spot. You can't fill a space that's not empty.

The things we have to let go to get to a place of peace within – well, it's easier said than done. Although the task is not easy and you may have to go through a time of solitude, you will be so grateful once you let the healing begin and you come out whole. If you find yourself in a season when everyone is pulling away from you, no matter how badly you want to chase behind them, know that it's necessary for where you're going. Take those moments and learn to enjoy yourself and treat yourself kindly. You never know how you may come out on the other side. I'm sure it will be love for the new you; I just know it!

Oftentimes, solitude can feel like the world may be against you, but what's really true is that the world is waiting for you. You need the time to cultivate all your gifts and talents to nourish your cravings for success. You can be a better help to those in your company when you are your truest self. Today is a good day to meet your potential and your future goal. Let that vision take you to your perfection.

A healthy body, a vivacious spirit and a mentally stable being. Whatever you desire, you have to see that up ahead.

You will have moments when you are content and standing still more than you're actually moving about. If it's in your vision to go to college, the path is discipline and good grades to achieve the goal. If the vision is joining the robotics team, the path is discipline, add to your knowledge and skill set, and developing your "team player" skills so your team can become champions.

If the vision is becoming an actress, the path is discipline, taking acting classes and studying the greats so that the world will one day remember your name. If the vision is becoming an actuarial scientist, the path is discipline, studying and pushing the limits concerning mathematical equations, probabilities and statistics.

Hopefully, you understand that your vision sets the discipline for what the preparation must look like. Without discipline, the vision only remains a vision with no movement toward the desired result. Your vision stays in a dream state, and it requires a shift from stagnation. The shift requires overcoming fears and making bold moves. The desire is in you for a reason. Because you have the ability to fulfill the desire, you have the full potential to get to a place that you will be equipped for.

FOCUS

LETTER 37
ALL THINGS HYGIENE

Dear Destiny,

Allow me to tell you all about *hygiene,* because if you hear it from one of your peers, there's no telling how the story would go.

People have stories that are good, bad, and indifferent, but it doesn't mean that you will have the same story or outcome. You must find out what's best for you when it comes to hygiene. Some requirements are the same for everyone: brush your teeth, floss and use mouthwash; shower, drink plenty of water, use deodorant and wash your hands often. Choose products that best suit you, and ask your doctor, pediatrician or dermatologist what's best for you.

When puberty hits, so many things begin to happen. Your body begins to develop, and your menstruation comes. Bad hygiene can cover up just how amazing a person really is. You can have a great personality, but if you have bad hygiene, that personality can often be buried so others won't get close enough to know you. You can be the best team player, but if your hygiene is not in check, other team members will miss what you can bring to the project. You're able to shoot the winning basket, but if your hygiene is not in check, it can cause you to cower from your full potential. We must bring it into alignment. Hygiene must be taken very seriously. If not taken care of, it can cause harsh rashes and infections that create extreme discomfort.

It's not a secret that individuals can be labeled by their behavior. Although it's absolutely unfair for one individual to point out another's failures or mediocrities, it's often done. Name calling can definitely be hurtful to an individual's self-esteem and self-worth, but we can also definitely try not to give an individual ammunition to attack us with.

Wash your hands properly to prevent the spread of germs and illnesses. Wash your hands with water and soap – wet your hands, lather, scrub, rinse and dry. Wash your hands before and after all activities.

Bathing is not a matter of if you want to do it – it's a must. Using a mild soap and shampoo is the only way to remove dirt and oil reduce your chances of acne or dandruff/dry scalp or infections. Wash your entire body including behind ears, underarms, groin, and your "southern region," in particular.

Choose your shampoo and/or conditioner based on your hair type. It's best to consult a dermatologist or professional hairstylist to understand how often you should wash your hair and what kind of products would work best. There are many things to consider if you have dry, oily, dandruff-rich hair, as well as texture – straight, coarse, curly, wavy, etc. In my teen years, dirty hair would set my acne into full outbreak. I finally understood the correlation and began to wash my hair weekly to keep the odds of a breakout at a minimum. In college, my roommates washed their hair daily.

For a teenager, deodorant is of utmost importance. When puberty begins, the sweat glands become more active and oftentimes, a tart smell comes along with it. This is why it's so important to change your clothes and socks after they've already been worn each day. On day two, the sweat is no joke. It will give your shoes and clothes a foul odor. If you're involved with sports, staying fresh is incredibly important for the team and your reputation. You don't want to walk in a room and have people smell you before you even walk by. Bad body odor of sweaty underarms and feet is not the best impression to leave.

Shaving is something you should receive a parent or guardian's permission to do if you're underage. Shaving is also based on preference. There are hair removal tools you can get so that you don't have to use a shaver and deal with a razor nicking you. A moisture rich body cream can keep your skin looking and feeling fabulous. Keep your lips moisturized by carrying some form of lip balm. Other essential items that could be great to have in arm's reach are hand sanitizer, Kleenex, mints or gum, and floss.

Taking care of your body is a great sign of self-discipline and self-care. When others see that you respect yourself and care enough to treat yourself well, you're teaching them how to treat you. You only get one body; a first impression and a lasting impression are important. Make them great.

LETTER 38
CREDIT

Dear Destiny,

I visited the campus of Saginaw Valley State University for an annual photoshoot for Delta Sigma Theta Sorority, Inc., Rho Mu Chapter. Before rushing off campus to eat, I had a moment to sit down with some students and talk finance. What I said to them was eye-opening – even for myself. Whether you're a first-generation college graduate or one of a successful handful of people in your family, you need good credit and a savings account when you cross the stage or you will pay. You must understand this and check on your credit score often.

Graduate as summa cum laude if you desire, but please don't pass up the opportunity to increase your knowledge about credit. This is something you must grasp. At least understand your credit and begin to build it. Money may rule the world, but it's definitely more helpful when it's coupled with good credit. Bad credit equals a bad interest rate, and good credit equals a good interest rate.

Have you ever seen the car commercials advertising a brand-new car at $300 a month and a small payment due at signing? That's definitely not for the person who has a low credit score. All those promises change once a customer cannot meet the minimal requirements.

What's a credit score you might ask, and why is it so important?
According to Experian, "Credit is the ability to borrow money or access goods or services with the understanding that you'll pay later." So, you're basically doing business using OPM – other people's money.

Lenders, merchants and service providers (known collectively as creditors) grant credit based on their confidence that you can be trusted to pay back what you borrowed, along with any finance charges that may apply. To the extent that creditors consider you worthy of their trust, you are said to be creditworthy, or to have "good credit."

The greatest thing about credit is that you can use someone else's money and build up a great score while your own money sits in your checking and savings accounts.

Here are a few helpful tips:

- There are three major credit bureaus: Experian, Equifax and TransUnion.
- The ultimate credit goal you want to achieve is an 850 FICO score.
- The most commonly used credit score models are Vantage Score 3.0 and FICO 8. These scoring models determine how "creditworthy" an individual is.

Credit Score Ranges (NerdWallet.com)

329-629 BAD

630-689 FAIR

690-719 GOOD

720-850 EXCELLENT

Five Credit Score Factors

Credit History - 35% (Make consistent timely payments)

Credit Utilization - 30% (Maintain a low credit card balance-10% or lower)

Length of credit history - 15% (Maintain long standing accounts)

New Credit - 10% (Apply for credit *only as needed*)

Credit Mix - 10% (Maintaining a good mix of revolving credit and installment loans generally represents less risk for a lender)

To get a great boost, consider asking your parents or guardians to add you to their credit cards as an authorized user that they have a great history on. This may give your score a good increase and you can share in their history of good credit. Even with credit, we should only purchase what we can afford to pay back ourselves.

We must educate ourselves and others about credit. Bad credit can prevent you from getting financed for a home, car, motorbike, insurance, utility companies, or in some cases, even a job. Credit is important. Remember that many factors change over the years, so continue to do your research.

Another major factor is having a bank account that includes checking and savings and encouraging others to do the same. You can see your money grow with compound interest, increase your basic math skills, save until you can afford, and never be caught off guard on a "rainy day." These are just a few tips to make your life a little easier. The sacrifice to maintain great credit can leave an amazing credit footprint, leading companies desiring to do business with you.

HOW TO MAKE EXTRA MONEY

Dear Destiny,

We are often taught to calculate forty hours a week, multiplied by $12.50, will get us a weekly gross pay of $500. Then, our net or "take-home" may be roughly $375. We are limited to how many hours we can work a week, but we are not limited to how many items we can sell day or night.

The Internet is the most powerful tool of our day. We can use it to promote the product or service of our choice and become wealthy overnight. It takes hard work, dedication and focus to achieve our goals, but it can be done sometimes even with a little adjustment and business mentoring.

Side hustles matter!

There is only one question you need to ask yourself: How bad do I want it? Anything you work at, you can totally make happen. You may have a 9-to-5 type of job, or you may have no job at all; but if you have the extra energy, going the extra mile may not be such a bad idea.

What about finding a product that can take people's lives to the next level? Something people can rarely live without, something people are constantly purchasing? There are many small businesses you can start right alongside school or work, and those may include:

- All-Natural Juices
- Logo Design
- House Painting
- Hair Bows
- Window Cleaning
- Babysitting
- Pet Sitting
- Candles
- Tutoring
- Cleaning Services
- Lemonade
- Virtual Assistant
- Business Coaching
- Closet Sorting
- All-Natural Soap

There are so many small business ideas. Instead of looking to calculate an hourly rate, think about purchasing an item online from a manufacturer at eight dollars ($8) per product including shipping, then in turn, selling it for $25. That's a $17 mark-up. If you sell just ten per day, that's $120 extra per day, and $840 per week, and possibly $3600 of additional income per month.

That's not bad for additional income. Start small and enjoy working your way up to the top. There's room for those who are determined to succeed. If you want something, work for it and watch it manifest.

LETTER 40
THE PERFECT
"WORK/LIFE BALANCE"

Dear Destiny,

My mother always says, "Too much of anything is not good for you." I am very guilty of being a "workaholic." I wake up working and go to bed doing the same thing, until one day, I found a balance and realized just how much living I was missing out on. One thing's for certain: You can't get time back. You may be able to reclaim lost time, but you will only be able to enjoy it at an older age. There's no going back.

You need a balance to enjoy the fruits of your labor. Although you may not have many things to be weighed, you have to consider how one thing can make you so much better in another area. Let me tell you about my "crashing" night after night.

I would go to bed without getting *ready* for bed. I would work all night until my poor laptop started to look like an enticing pillow and my eyes were too heavy to keep open. I had to learn to call it quits and get ready for bed with no cords and electronics. It is a discipline I still continue to practice, and it has made a world of difference.

Make time for the things you love and the people you love. You are in control of your own life, as well as your own schedule.

If you fail to plan, someone will be happy to come and plan your life in a way that will benefit them. You have to manage your time well or you will always be available to deplete your energy, giving it over to someone or something. There's a balance to life; you deserve to play hard if you work hard. After basics are out of the way such as homework, studying and work, give time to relaxation and self-care.

Be careful not to make yourself always available. Growing up, I was the best babysitter in the world, if you asked me. I had kids with me every summer, and the parents would be so happy because their children would return knowing loads of information. I taught kids how to read, write, count, spell and play fun games.

One summer, as always, I was gearing up to babysit and my mom said I couldn't do it. Before I could ask her why, she started explaining that people will allow you to do everything they need you to do. She told me that it was important to have healthy boundaries and to make sure I was enjoying my life. Babysitting was incredibly fun, but had I put myself first, I would've chosen my summer activities, had fun with kids my age and gotten better at some of my talents and skills. I would have left additional time open for babysitting.

If babysitting is your full-time job, something you're doing for work, you may have to make it a priority. However, still make time for yourself after work to do the things you enjoy for a great work/life balance.

When you give too much of yourself without a balance, you can become bitter about opportunities your peers take on. Although the opportunity may be open to all, you may not have taken advantage of it, thinking and placing others above an opportunity you have for your success. It's not selfish to take advantage of the things that can make you better and help position you to reach back and be the same blessing to someone else.

I manage my time and don't let any tasks run together. Sleep doesn't mean television, and exercise time doesn't mean snacking and texting. The new schedule I have helps me to appreciate work better. When I'm at work, I'm present and full of energy. I'm not crying on the inside, wishing I was asleep. I check emails when the time is appropriate, and I'm not scrolling during personal conversations with someone who deserves my undivided attention. Work has its proper time and relaxation has its own. I stopped apologizing for going on vacation. I've learned to put down the work and pick up the phone for only selfies. We have to live our best life now, but it has to be a balance to the hard work because tomorrow is not promised, and time waits for no one!

BALANCE

FAMILY
FRIENDS
SCHOOL
HEALTH
FUN

LETTER 41
DEALING WITH LOSS

Dear Destiny,

When you tell someone, "See you tomorrow," that's exactly what you mean, without ever considering that moment might not come. One of the most life-altering experiences I've ever had was losing a loved one – my brother. It took me about 10 years to get back to a state of ease, but I've never actually been the same. The hardest part of loving a person is to one day lose that person, understanding how awesome we are to have the privilege and ability to love.

I went to the mall to grab a hat. I was so tempted to exit the freeway and switch my day around and go to the salon first where my family typically gathered on a Saturday morning. However, I followed my original plan and missed an opportunity to see my brother for the final time.

I got the call on the third floor of the mall and swiftly made my way to the exit. Although I was moving fast, I was grasping on to every bit of faith that had ever been deposited in me. I knew I would make it in time to check my brother's status and to realize it was just a scare. It was far from a scare.

Once I arrived, I grabbed this book that was always in arm's reach. I ran inside and many family members and friends pointed me to where I could find my mom, aunt and siblings. We prayed and prayed and prayed. The doctor returned, as I believed he had come in before. He then told my mom, "We did everything we could…." The rest of the words were irrelevant for that time. I was still hopeful. Maybe they made a mistake. Maybe there was some type of mix-up.

I was being strong – or trying to be. They told us we could come back to see him. We went and he was just lying there – almost as though he was asleep. It was as if he was going to jump up and try to scare me as usual. The room grew very still, and he never moved. I told him I would take the Lord's will, but other than that, he should get up. See, we always pranked each other, but reality kept trying to squeeze its way in to let me know that this was not a prank. I just had no room to accept otherwise because my faith wouldn't let me see otherwise. The clock ticked, and I grew faint.

I went inside that room physically and didn't come out mentally for ten long years. Years that I lived but relationships I could've gambled because my trust and expectations of others grew faint.

Life took more than my brother; I lost my best friend, one of my first teachers, the person who would make me sit with my legs folded, close my eyes and think "mind over matter." Too many pranks to number and the worst thing he could've ever taught me was, "Never let them see you cry." I think that's the funniest because no matter how emotional I was, I would let it stay inside and never respond outwardly the way I really felt. Although I hid my emotions, it gave me time to process the matter – a blessing and a curse.

When a person grieves, they often go through five main emotional phases: denial and isolation, anger, bargaining, depression, and finally, acceptance. Somehow, I was going through what felt like all five stages of grief at once. People who are grieving do not necessarily go through the stages in the same order or experience all of them.

I lived with so many questions and the teacher who would answer my questions was gone. I just didn't understand why he couldn't wait until I got there! This was the biggest blow I'd ever had to take; nothing could phase me from this point. I was numb to everything from that point. I still had many incredible moments in my life, but more often than not, I felt a huge void knowing Paris was not here.

I had an amazing pastor who came to my family's aide and provided us with the warmest support. He'd taught us prior that, "You never care how much a person knows until you know how much a person cares." Bishop Elect Marvin Winans shifted his schedule to accommodate the funeral arrangements. We stand forever grateful!

Everything about the person I lost stayed with me and my family. The great thing about it all, however, is that my brother left us with tons of memories and beautiful children for us to love and hold a little bit tighter. My brother, James Jr., became twice a brother and I'm forever grateful for his love and support. Every day we heal, and every day we grow stronger together.

Twelve years later, I had an "A-ha!" moment. I had to be broken before I got better, and I accepted that. I had so much bottled up inside and, because I knew it was not the most positive, I had to get it out, even if it was followed by an apology. I had to let everyone who was close to me know that I was going through a process of healing. I disconnected from my places and positions of comfort, mustered up the strength to speak out about things and again began to make sure I had no toxic relationships. It was worth it in the end. The feeling on this side is much better.

On this side of "going through," I'm definitely stronger, wiser, and better. I didn't see the need to compare my hurt to anyone else's, but I talked with my good friend, Theo, who explained to me that he lost more than one sibling, and yet the smile on his face and his eagerness to win in life motivated me all the more. I learned that we all face challenges. It's just a part of life in a world that doesn't stop, so we have to find a way to adjust, cry, laugh, and smile. But don't get stuck! We have to keep moving.

While I'm on this subject, let me quickly interject a few funeral etiquette tips. If you know of a close friend or family member who passed away, it's more than kind to go pay your respects unless the funeral is private. Attend the funeral on time. If there's a guestbook, make sure you sign it to let the host know you attended. This information is typically used to send thank you notes at a later time. A sympathy card is appropriate to bring along; you may not get the opportunity to introduce yourself should you not know the family. Make sure you place your phone on silent, limit talking, and if you become overwhelmed with emotion, step out. *Don't take pictures!* If you give remarks during the service, follow the rules and keep it brief.

Love those who are close to you. Reach out and check on people, both strong and weak. Tomorrow is uncertain, but today you can make full use of your ability to love. Thank those who think of you and go the extra mile with those who would drop anything for you.

LETTER 42
KNOWLEDGE MAKES YOU
AN INDEPENDENT THINKER

Dear Destiny,

What I know for sure is that a book can open up your mind to the world. The more information we have, the more power we have to excel. Knowledge is wealth. If you can see it and understand it, you can carry it out and accomplish it. Books give strategies and information that will save you a great deal of time and research in many areas. If you want to go far in life, read, read and read some more. You can open your mind to a world of unlimited possibilities.

As an adolescent, my favorite book was *I Know Why the Caged Bird Sings,* written by the late Dr. Maya Angelou, whose wisdom I carry in my heart. Her life story lit something in me that could never be put out. I loved the book titled *Beloved,* written by the late Toni Morrison, and the many V.C. Andrews books – the *Landry* series, to be exact. These books shaped my mind and introduced me to the true power of thought. They took me places I'd never gone and challenged my mind to paint pictures I never thought I could conjure up.

Without experience, we are limited to our single story. Lacking the ability to read and see life through another person's eyes can make us callus and narrow-minded. Another person's testimony or story can help you overcome and be inspired to push past a similar trial when presented. You can look back and it can come to mind; if "Saundra" made it over, so can I.

One's early adventures are often found in reading. Your eyes can be opened to a life that someone paid royally to live. You get an opportunity to live through them. The ability to travel from a bonfire in the woods of California with the funniest friends a girl could ever have, to swimming in the Pacific Ocean amongst the Coral Reef in Australia. Through books, you can travel and nearly touch, taste, feel and see with your imagination. I traveled around the world when I read Dr. Maya Angelou's stories. I traveled as I sat right on my couch, wrapped in a blanket with a fresh fire going. Books are a great form of exposure.

What we don't know or read can hurt us. Human beings are born with various blood types. Did you know that there are certain foods that are better for you based on your blood type alone? Just because you don't know pertinent information about your health doesn't mean you won't suffer the consequences for not knowing. This is also something you can consider when it comes to the law. If you break the law, you can suffer the consequences, whether you were aware of the law or not. Stay alert. Read, learn, grow, and *go*.

I'm sure you know how important an education is. People will sacrifice their life savings often for their children to become educated and create a path for the entire family. One of the keys to a successful education is the ability to read. Value your ability to read. If it's an area in which you struggle, I'm so sure that the more you read, the better you will get at it. If you have a little difficulty pronouncing words, I encourage you to try some free online lessons. It takes time to become an amazing reader, but once you achieve this goal, you will never be the same.

LETTER 43
CLEAR COMMUNICATION WITH A BALANCE

Dear Destiny,

"You are so aggressive," I told my friend.

"Why are you calling me bad names?" she responded.

"Because you keep trying to boss me around," I said, giggling. Although she was aggressive, what I said was not intended to hurt her feelings. But I thought if she could stop and recognize her harsh behavior toward me, she would understand what I was feeling. Sometimes, our ways can be rooted in our culture, habits and how we are raised.

It's important to get to know someone's intentions. Maybe a person's intentions are not to boss you around and tell you what to do; maybe it's just their way of being direct. You may not like how they are conveying the message, but that's okay. Here is where we have to learn patience and kindly tell a person at a better time that you didn't like the tone they take with you, or you didn't like the way they talked about someone else. Ask them also if there's anything *you* are doing they are not comfortable with and let them feel free to mention it. Sometimes, what's fun and games for one friend may not equally workout for another; it's good to be mindful of that.

No need to be upset over what makes us different. It's part of the growing process of friends and getting to know people. You have to steer them in the right direction and remember that others may have some of the same expectations for you. Talk things over and come to an agreement. People may not change overnight, and if it's not abusive, give them a chance to take their behavior off "default." Come to an agreement that both sides can live with and enjoy your journey.

There are no promises regarding a person changing because you've asked them to. You may have to ask yourself what exactly you *can* deal with. There are too many factors when considering people and emotions. After all, sometimes even the slightest things can cause people to quickly change their attitudes. You want to always keep a positive attitude.

What image do you want to come to an individual's mind when they think of you? How do you want people to associate you? I want to be associated with grace, class and integrity. A brand is how someone identifies you or your business. When you see the golden arches, you can associate that with McDonalds and those amazing golden fries. When people see you, what would you like for them to see or think?

I went back to school to pursue my master's degree and gained a greater level of knowledge and strategy to become the greatest educator for the present generation. I plan to also receive my doctorate degree in educational technology and develop a level of research as to the importance of doing away with antiquated teaching models and introduce teacher education innovation paired with technology.

Consistency is important. When it comes to you and how others view you, you can be in charge of your emotions and your brand. Communication is vital; you have to discern the proper time to tell someone how you feel. In front of a crowd may not be the best place. If you genuinely want to see change, it's best not to try to embarrass someone even if what they are doing is making you uncomfortable. Walk away if needed. Don't blurt things out and don't say everything that comes to mind, but instead, think before you speak. There is a time and a place for everything. Ask yourself how you would want someone to handle the situation if it was you? Consider your image and never let someone take you out of character.

LETTER 44
YOU ARE LOVED!

Dear Destiny,

Thank you for allowing me to love you and share my thoughts with you along your journey. I know I say it often, but I'm excited about what the future holds for you and even for what life has already given you. You're a gift to this world, and I want you to know that you are full of purpose. It's alright to pour out sunshine each day, spreading your peace and love amongst those you come in contact with. The good energy you give out will definitely gravitate back your way.

I may not be here one day to see all the awards, or the notable mentions tied to your great deeds you might be honored for, but beyond a shadow of a doubt, dear daughter, I'm proud of you. I'm proud of you because you had a desire to hear wisdom and build from your mistakes. You've taken alternatives for solving problems into consideration and worked, or are working, through situations that seem insurmountable. I'm proud of you for taking a stand for what's right, even if you have to go about it alone.

You've opened up your mind to new ideas and strategies. You've opened your heart to care for and support others while remaining true to yourself and encompassing beautiful strength. You understand the strength of forgiveness and moving on with your life. You owe it to yourself to discover how amazing your life will turn out for the better.

You will make it through every trial and through the days when you feel like the wind has been knocked out of you and the rug has been pulled from under you. Sometimes, you only need to look back to be reminded just how far you've come and your ability to make such great progress. I want you to know you're loved.

> *You're beautiful just the way God created you, and*
> *You're certainly an artist's greatest masterpiece.*
> *You're an architect's greatest and strongest structure.*
> *You're a politician's greatest triumph.*
> *You're loved like a composer's greatest piece of music.*
> *You're loved like a writer's favored poem.*
> *You're loved like a poet's most impressive ballad.*
> *You're loved like a chef's favorite dish.*
> *You're loved like a beautiful forecast on an important day.*
> *You're an athlete's greatest victory.*
> *You're my greatest accomplishment...*

... and I wish, above all things, that you would live and that you would do it out loud with a smile. Dream the dream, become everything you desire, write the vision, write the book, and reach for the stars. Reach boldly, knowing who you are, which is half the battle in life. I want you to know you're light.

You're light that gives meaning to an otherwise dark space.
You're intelligent and your ability to make wise decisions
benefits you and those around you.
You're gorgeous, unique, and one of a kind.
You have the superpower of being the only person
that knows every single detail and feeling concerning yourself.
You're humble, you open the door for yourself
but kindly let others through.
You're talented and your gift will cause many doors to open to you.

Write, Type, Record

If you're anything like me, great thoughts just come to mind randomly when you're far away from a notebook to jot the thoughts down. These great ideas are so necessary to write down, so when the time comes, you can put them to work. If you have access to a cell phone, there is typically an app for note taking. Write your God thoughts down and when you get a moment follow up on them. They help pave the way to solving world problems and paving the road pointing toward your destiny.

Reminder

You Are

LIGHT

INTELLIGENT

GORGEOUS

HUMBLE

TALENTED

LETTER 45
PUSH THE ENVELOPE/
TAKE THE LEAP

Dear Destiny,

You don't have to live with regrets. Life is your greatest teacher; we live and learn. The things that we struggle with are so necessary for our purpose, and how we go through them is of most importance. Writing this book was so important to me because so often my friends say, "If I knew then what I know now, I wouldn't have made this or that mistake." So, my job is to teach you through the mistakes we adults have already made.

If you mess up, learn from it. It's never too late to start over; but as I mentioned before, time is of the essence. The more shoulders you are able to climb on, the quicker you're able to get to the top. Understanding how those shoulders got stable will keep you from falling when hit.

You need to take great strides to take your thoughts and ideas to the next level. Initially, life seems so long, and you have so many years ahead of you, but before you know it, you'll find yourself in your late 60's. While that is a beautiful age full of wisdom, you may find that you don't have the same energy you had at 18. So use your youth while you have it. Enjoy it, work smart, and defy the odds. Once you find those who have paved the way for you, jump on their shoulders, learn from them and complete the work. Take the research to the next level, build the school, write the book, spread knowledge, and complete the dream.

What's holding you back from achieving your dreams? There were many who came before you who redefined the boundaries and shook up the world. Let their lives speak to you – like the great life of Shirley Chisholm, the first African American to run for president of the United States of America on a democratic ticket in 1972. Although the odds were stacked against her being a black woman, she ran for president anyway. She was called names and was told that she didn't belong; and yet, she didn't let that stop her. Stand on her mighty shoulders. Study her life and go after a seat in congress if you desire. Fight injustice and teach, but whatever you do, go after your dreams and succeed.

Let the life of Folorunsho Alakija, the wealthiest African woman in Nigeria, speak to you. Mrs. Alakija is a Nigerian philanthropist and businesswoman who's involved in the oil, fashion and real estate industries. Her first company was a fashion label which had customers such as the wife of former Nigerian president, Ibrahim Babangida. She was awarded an oil prospecting license in 1993 from the Nigerian government that was later converted to an oil mining lease. She serves as the executive vice-chairman of Famfa Oil Limited. Mrs. Alakija is ranked by Forbes as the richest woman in Nigeria with an estimated net worth of $1 billion.

Alexandria Ocasio-Cortez is a 30-year-old member of the U.S. House of Representatives from New York's 14th District. She won the Democratic Party's primary election on June 26, 2018.

She defeated a 10-term incumbent and became the youngest woman to serve in the United States Congress. Ocasio-Cortez graduated cum laude from Boston University. Her jobs prior to running for Congress were waitressing and bartending.

Malala Yousafzai's human rights advocacy for the education of women and children in Pakistan led her to become the youngest Nobel Prize laureate. During a time when the local Taliban banned girls from attending school, Malala stood for what she believed. Malala's father was an inspiration to her. He was a humanitarian, and her family ran a chain of schools. Her activism nearly cost her life. In retaliation for her activism, Malala and two other girls were shot by a Taliban gunman in 2012 while on the bus. The attempt to assassinate the girls was unsuccessful, and Malala lived to tell her story.

There was an international outpouring of support for Malala, and her story appeared in The New York Times. From there, the story caught the attention of many. Malala went on to be nominated for the International Children's Peace Prize by activist Desmond Tutu. The 2015 issue of Time Magazine featured her as one of the most influential people globally. She was awarded honorary Canadian citizenship and became the youngest person to address the House of Commons of Canada. Talk about defying odds!

Prove it to yourself that you can be the first, and you can be the best. Convince them that you have what it takes, that you have the greatest idea to bring about world change. You have the best product or service that they can't live without. Persuade them to jump on the bandwagon, and lock in. I totally believe in you! Stand up for what you believe in and be happily, unapologetically you.

Sometimes, you have to take chances to achieve your goals and you must show up. Bishop T.D. Jakes once said, "Anything you don't engage in you can't change" and "It's not the things you did right that taught you the most but the things you did wrong." The valuable lessons teach you to get up and do it again seamlessly without flaw. Just remember, take chances with opportunities – not your life.

LETTER 46
THE PATH

Dear Destiny,

My mother always instilled in us the importance of not being in the wrong place at the wrong time. She told us, "Birds of a feather flock together" and, "Looking at the people around you says a lot about who you will become if you haven't yet become." With a mother like mine, those words will stick in your mind and return during the perfect moment. We couldn't get anything past my mother. She's always had a quick wit, but rarely ever raised her voice.

My mom was always so good at knowing exactly which child did what. If it was a dirty dish, it was absolutely Jr.; if there was food left on the table, it was Paris. If the plate was full and never been touched, it was me. The girls had their fair share of being irresponsible, because no matter how clean the bathroom was, it would still be considered to be in disarray because Jamea never unplugged the curling iron. She also drew beautiful murals on the back of the doors. She was such a great artist that it took the sting out of her getting in trouble because it was too beautiful to punish her. Donna always tied up the phone lines and Keke always had somewhere to go with a group of friends. It was a busy house, and there was never a dull moment.

My mother always tried to help us discover the path we were on. She would challenge us to look at those we surrounded ourselves with and ask us how we fit in. She never pretended for one moment that only our friends could have a negative impact on us, but that we also had the ability to push our weaknesses off on others. If my mother could point out to us what we have to offer this world, surely, we know our own strengths and weaknesses firsthand. You must come to a place where you realize the road you are traveling down and where it begins to split off from everyone else. Should you begin to head down the wrong path and lose yourself, pull back.

Why do you choose the friends you choose? Do they add value to your life? What attracts you to them? Oftentimes, an individual's ways and habits will rub off on those closest to them. After all, if you're hanging around someone who only indulges in bad behavior, and you are constantly seeing the same behavior, you open yourself up to two opportunities: join them or be disgusted by it. But why would you continue to stay around it when people might soon associate you with the same behaviors? There are many people and habits you must avoid on your path that will send you backwards. You must steer away from drugs and gateway drugs (drugs that lead to more potent drugs), prostitution, alcoholism, smoking, stealing, lying, cheating, gossiping and the like.

The reason you want great, healthy relationships is because iron sharpens iron. Having someone who can bring the best out of you and vice versa on this path is priceless. So, remember that you are in charge of the path you take in life. There are so many, but most importantly, the one less traveled is typically the one that leads to success. Don't follow the people. Lead them.

LETTER 47
STAY READY

Dear Destiny,

I received a call from Char Goolsby informing me that Her Excellency, Tebelelo Mazile Seretse, had again come to the Motor City and invited us to a strategic business meeting pertaining to doing work in the beautiful country of Botswana. Although my business was doing fairly well, I wasn't ready for expansion.

Last year, the phenomenal Meagan Good-Franklin told such an amazing story about preparation that I carry close to my heart. Her husband had been working out as he normally does and was encouraging her to join him. Meagan said she pushed herself to exercise and it wasn't something she looked forward to. She walked up and down the driveway for starters and slowly got to the point where she could add a little intensity to this new way of life. She had gotten to the point where she was joining her husband for a workout session at the gym and soon it became second nature to her. But that's not the amazing part.

Shortly afterward, Meagan was offered to play a role in a Hollywood film that she had to be in tip-top shape for. If you've ever even seen a picture of Mrs. Good-Franklin, you'd see that she was serving pure beauty and looking like a picture of perfect health.

She was able to take the role with confidence and immediately understood the importance of "being ready." When you "stay ready," you don't have to "get ready." This spoke so loudly to me. There are so many opportunities that can be attached to your business and plans. If you always lay things out, you can just open the door and walk in when the opportunities come. You have to stay ready, speak it into existence, and really expect it to manifest.

Since that moment, I've been ready – mind body and soul. Let the opportunities come. I've moved from my comfort zone and you must move from yours. Stretch yourself to the place from which you need to lead. The best way to measure where you need to be is to determine where you are currently and look back at the previous years. Has your attitude improved? How about your work ethic or your spending habits? Do you see progress?

It's time to become the amazing person you were created to be. Step into your rightful role as bold, brave, courageous, intrepid, valiant, and valorous. There's a place for you in this world. The world needs what you have to give, so please show up because you never know who might be watching you and encouraged by your tenacity to succeed.

LETTER 48
YOU HAVE 50,000 COACHES

Dear Destiny,

I'm not the only one rooting for you and your success. I'm not the only one who believes that one day, all your dreams will come to fruition. A few years back, I helped my great friend Jillian Blackwell over the summer. Jill is always bringing fun and interesting ideas to the community, reaching out for her colleagues' support to make any project a huge success. This particular summer, Jill was working with Microsoft and decided to sign me up to help facilitate a youth coding class.

While each day we take part in the complex but incredible world of coding through computer software, social media, websites, apps and such, it's so empowering to put a young person behind the wheel and allow them to be in control of creating something that can revolutionize the world.

So many doors have been opened in the area of Science, Technology, Engineering and Math (S.T.E.M.) for young girls and women alike. Coding is a form of STEM.

I was so honored to host a girls coding workshop at the Microsoft store that summer as well. I love to see people become educated and enlightened about anything that causes them to bring change to the world. Creation is in full support of you, and there are so many paths you can take to become successful. Many are also willing to help you get there if you're first found helping yourself.

The world is within reach and you have unlimited access through the World Wide Web. Anything you want to create, you have the ability to get a better understanding of by researching it and finding those who have engaged in the business before you. We talked about the benefit of books and reading in past letters, which plays a large part in excelling and making your dreams a reality. You have the opportunity to create and execute if you focus on what you want. What you have to give up pales in comparison to what you will gain.

I love movies with educational settings. Two of my favorite movies are *The Theory of Everything* and *Akeelah and the Bee*. In *Akeelah and the Bee,* a young South Los Angeles student named Akeelah became the Scripps National Spelling Bee champion. Along the way, she lost friends and even her spelling coach. She felt alone. She told her mother of her discouragement and her mother brought her comfort by telling her that she was not alone and her community stood behind her. Although Akeelah's determination got her as far as she did, she needed assistance to get past the finish line. Akeelah's mom told her that she had "50,000 coaches." When she opened her eyes to what her mother had told her, she saw that there were so many people helping and cheering her on.

There will be a time when your moment arrives and you have to step up to the plate. There are many teachers who are there to cheer you on, though sometimes our focus is gauged on the wrong individuals. Open your eyes and look for those who are there to help.

66

**You have
50,000 COACHES**
starting with me ♥

99

LETTER 49
EVERYTHING MY FATHER
TAUGHT ME

Dear Destiny,

I can't tell you from a man's perspective what's best to look out for in friendships, relationships and dating. Special thanks to my "mom," Dr. Cindy Trimm-Tomlinson who so effortlessly freed me by saying, "Go talk with your dad." I went and had a moment with one of my favorite individuals, a well-respected man of wisdom, my godfather, Mr. Russell Tomlinson, who I affectionately call "Dad." He's selfless. He's put so much into raising his daughters that they in turn exude that same love and wisdom to their own children and husbands. I wanted to share his wisdom with you and I thank my sisters, Lakeya, Alicia, and Stephanie for sharing their amazing father with me.

Perhaps you have a similar father or father figure present in your life; this letter will just be confirmation of some of the discussions you might have had with him regarding relationships. But if your father was *not* involved in your life, or he was present, but not emotionally available, I hope this letter will yield the answers to the many questions you may have.

My dad shared so much wisdom in the area of relationships that it even helped me reevaluate and think on some things. I asked my dad a series of questions pertaining to life and the advice he would give to an adolescent, or young adult, woman who wanted to pursue healthy relationships. Some things have changed since he's raised his daughters, but he's well caught up with the times we live in now. I asked about the triumphs, pitfalls (what to watch out for), relationship goals, strategies, tactics and what one has to offer and receive in a relationship. The only way to find out how a man thinks is to ask a man.

Q: From a man's perspective, what would you want your daughter to know about relationships?
A: I would want my daughters to know what the model man looks like. By the time my daughters choose their relationships, they will already have an idea of what their choice should be based on – that model or prototype. The information should be conveyed and confirmed from the mother and the father; if the children are present, they learn through watching how the father treats the mother. When there are no consistent parents in the picture, we have to include stories conveyed of the model including qualities that represent the positive father figure so all daughters know what they deserve in any relationship.

Q: What does that model look like?
A: He's strong for her so he can carry her if she gets weak physically, emotionally, mentally or financially;

He's confident,

He's a respectful communicator,

He's a leader,

He's a listener,

He's honest and forthright,

He's a gentleman: he will assist her up the steps, open the car door, pull her chair out and pick up what she puts down, helps her to remove her coat, and he's comfortable in her presence as she is in his.

The right model will cause the young lady to prepare herself accordingly, based on the type of male she looks to meet. She now has an idea as to what she desires in a man. As she ages, she must begin to practice the art of patience so her wants can be accommodated. The young lady who knows her worth will expect the man to open the door for her, to be considerate. She's looking for someone to handle her in the way her father said she should be handled.

There are things she should also withhold, such as sharing finances and giving expensive gifts. Be careful not to allow people to pay large sums of money because they will create an obligation to involve you in ways you may not have been prepared for. If the person has invested greatly, they eventually would want something in return. Determining boundaries early on and revisiting them can assist in making sure two people are on the same page. As a young lady, if you want to preserve your virtue, don't get involved in receiving expensive gifts within a relationship.

What a daughter should be prepared to present or give away in a relationship, if he's good enough for her, is her time, company, conversation, admiration and attraction. You have to protect yourself when the dating is too private; you open up the door for a greater temptation. The dating must be aboveground and if possible, he needs to talk to your parents. Include supervision when you go out, or join a group of friends that you're accountable to. No one does it perfectly, but what I've learned is that if you give people an opportunity to do it right, even if they stray, they have the ability to get back on the track.

What makes a male assume a woman is desperate is measured through observation and reputation. Growing up, there was no mystery as to who was desperate. It starts off with observation, then people will testify to her reputation. Avoid being tagged by your peers because it will follow you beyond your high school 20th year class reunion.

I'm going to pause this amazing chat with my dad and tell you this short story that will bring all the more clarity as to why you should be careful not to do things purposely in your youth that will attach a stigma to your name possibly for the rest of your days.

Mrs. Green-Woods shared this story with my etiquette students. Although she was uncomfortable telling it, she knew it was necessary. There was another young girl named Susan who attended the same high school. She wanted to be popular and liked, so she decided to indulge in sexual acts with a few male classmates. Shortly after, those same classmates began to spread this information around the school and it tarnished her reputation. They later labeled her, "Slutty Susan." What an awful name.

Every young female must avoid being gullible. Don't believe everything someone tells you, and if you don't know or understand something, always ask for time to think about it. Check in with someone who is much wiser than you. Mrs. Green-Woods shared that even years later, it's still hard to shake from one's mind that handle they placed on Susan's name.

Back to my chat with my dad!

Your mom has always taught you to let your name be associated with great things. When people think of you, what thoughts do you want to pop into their minds? Popularity does not equal quality, and if you value and desire a good name, work for it. Being confident does not make you arrogant. Knowing who you are carries a beautiful essence; the feeling is connected to being grateful. The thought is pure and not boastful.

It is said that women date men who are like their father. Stay woke and don't date men who have personality traits like the bad father. If your father didn't have great traits and didn't lead in a positive manner, although there may be a magnetic pull to connect with someone with the same characteristics, you have to make a sound decision to go the other way. That's why I thought it was so important to include the wisdom of my dad, Mr. Russell Tomlinson, because where we lack in our life experiences, I believe God makes up for it in the people He sends into our lives, especially the ones who possess great wisdom and knowledge.

Studies show a girl with a supportive father who is present physically and emotionally is less likely to have sex at an early age and become a teen parent. Because she values what she wants, like education and success, she waits longer to get married and have children. Linda Nielsen, a professor of educational and adolescent psychology at Wake Forest University in North Carolina, writes on this on the Family Studies site:

If you find yourself liking someone who possesses the qualities you feel are that of the model gentleman and he hasn't approached you, it's fine if you at least have a conversation with him. Through that, a young man can typically pick up that you like him or you're open to be a friend of his. Attraction is first sight, verbal interaction, and even touch (shaking hands).

Q: Is there a safe age to date?
A: First things first: what do your grades look like? Are you keeping up in school? Do you know what your priorities are between school, extracurricular activities and responsibilities? Dating comes with a level of maturity not age. Ask yourself, are you ready to date? If a 16-year-old wants to date but suffers with low self-esteem issues, it's probably not a good time to start dating because she has some internal things to work through. Her esteem needs to be built up. If she only finds what she needs in a guy, she would lean too heavily on him. This can oftentimes make for an unhealthy relationship. We want what guys tell us to be affirming, meaning that it confirms what we already know, and in humility we respond and say, "Thank you." If you are mature, you can wait until the right time to date.

The first thing in dating is to define the relationship, setting boundaries. After you've asked your parents' permission, share your expectations with the guy. Some things we may have listed may not be things he's been taught, so kindly share these social graces and allow him to implement them in the dating process. Dating at 16 often starts with supervision. Then when ready, your parents will possibly allow you to make it a group thing, set with a curfew and healthy boundaries. You probably shouldn't be alone if you're still in high school. You're never too strong to fall, especially when you leave room for error such as staying overnight and being left alone.

Dating is just another part of life and, at a young age, know you have your entire life ahead of you. Have fun, enjoy the company of others, think smart and share great stories. *Most importantly,* keep your clothes on. You will do so much living and so much learning, and you will contribute great things to this world. I've learned that everything rises and falls on relationships. Be careful how you enter them and, if need be, how you exit them as well.

LETTER 50
MASTERING YOUR FUTURE

Dear Destiny,

So, what's the future looking like for you? Are you ready to go after your dreams and dance with the stars? What does the path look like and how do you plan to navigate through the halls of academia to get there? What path are you going to choose?

Preparation prevents poor progress. You have to decide where you want to go and lay out the path that will be the best fit for your destination and, perhaps, your learning style. When the goal is to be the brightest and best, you must be willing to go up against the best to stay the course.

There are various colleges you can attend, some more rigorous than others. I attended Northwood University, which is a private university. I felt like I went to class for longer hours than high school. Although my friends who attended other universities enjoyed their simple two-semesters-per-school-year, we were working triple time on trimesters and longer days. Even so, my education was so rewarding and college was amazing. I knew that what I learned could be applied in the real world. I marched across the stage and right into a job that I was able to secure, not just because of my schooling, but because of the entire package we were taught to present: The Northwood Idea.

My degree took me beyond a job. I began businesses as well. You can always start a business; but you must learn how to manage and grow that business. You must keep your finances in order, and a college degree or vocational program could be extremely helpful. It's true that many succeed and never step foot into a college or university, but that number is slim compared to the number of individuals who go and are more likely to be able to choose their own path. Often when you fail to become educated or are even self-taught, people choose for you.

I would often tell my students when you're trained for a position, or have the knowledge and capacity to learn a job or business, you are an asset. You can present your gifts and talents and be offered positions. You can be so great at a skill that a company will let others go to bring you on board. When you have zero skills and no capacity to learn such a skill, you only can go with jobs that are open that you will typically over qualify for. This is when we realize if we set ourselves up for success, we get to choose.

I went back to school to pursue and gain a greater level of knowledge and strategy. I wanted to become a greater asset so my knowledge would increase my worth and be considered a reliable source. I asked teachers how their students connect and how to adapt teaching style based on their learning style. I continue to return to the classroom both as a teacher and a student. I'm a lifetime learner and teacher. Education is a vehicle and a tool. The need for technology, finance and business within communities is my fuel. You may desire an occupation that you need a special skill to complete. There are many skilled trades that you can learn in college, technical school or specialized training courses. This is an opportunity to develop the same specific skill with a certification versus a four-year degree. Whatever path you choose, make it count.

HEY, YOUNG WORLD, STAY WOKE

Dear Destiny,

The feeling of knowing you're safe is one of the most comforting, peaceful feelings an individual can have. Everyone deserves to live in a safe home, attend a safe school and work within a safe work environment. Sometimes the places in which we live and operate may not function at our ideal level, which is an environment that protects us from dysfunction and doesn't expose us to great danger. This may not be the easiest conversation to have, but it must be had. I will attempt to break it down as much as possible.

I would like to believe that people do not want to be put in harm's way, but what if you reside in a place that is not so safe? How do you create a place of peace and rest in the midst of turmoil? If you live in a place where there is a lot of activity going on, such as parents arguing, overcrowding, family members talking down at you as well as disrespecting you, it's important to make room for yourself mentally, spiritually and physically. Although, maybe not all at once due to a possibility of limited space and resources.

Find a safe space. If there is no room physically for you to steal away, create a space mentally. Take the time and create a

Destiny Journal. Make your safe haven through writing or drawing and live there. Create and carve out the future plan that will give you a better future and hold tight to the plan. Although there are many unfavorable outcomes when young people grow up in dysfunction and experience traumatic events, you can break through the statistics and steer toward a path of success and joy versus one of disappointment, fear, rejection and depression.

If the issues going on within an individual's home includes sexual assault or abuse, reach out to a mandated reporter immediately. Mandated reporters are those who often come in contact with youth or those who can be labeled as vulnerable. These individuals must report any forms of abuse or neglect. In your everyday life, you may encounter teachers, principals, counselors, school bus drivers or a Girl Scout troop leader; these are all mandated reporters. Never be afraid to report the truth. No matter how the "chips may fall," if someone has molested or abused you, or someone you know, *report it!*

If no one has ever done you any harm, never let someone influence you to say something different. Never report a lie or accuse anyone of doing something they have not done to draw attention to yourself. If you are constantly in need of attention, there are other ways to work through this matter without making up false stories.

There are people who are not in the best frame of mind and they desire to manipulate adolescents and young adults alike. They desire to abuse them and/or kidnap them for various reasons. Alert! Sex trafficking is at an all-time high, so let's try our absolute best to escape it by following safety precautions.

You must choose wisely when it comes to who you can trust. Unfortunately, you can't trust everyone. Maybe you've grown up in a home where those closest to you have shown that they can be trusted and they haven't brought any harm to you – that's good! On the flipside, maybe you've grown up in a home where the same people you trusted betrayed that trust and abused you. That's very unfortunate and I'm sorry that you've endured that, and we won't let the situation rob you of your future.

Do you have to live a life of fear, thinking every moment of the day that someone is going to come after you? No, but you do need to realize that you must make the best decisions concerning where to go and what events to attend based on your safety and security. Are you going with people who will make sure you're safe? Will you do the same to make sure they are safe? Always make sure you're getting in and out of a vehicle in a well-lit area if you're alone. If you meet someone on the Internet, beware of "stranger danger" and steer clear of meeting up with this person. Furthermore, beautiful one, anytime you do meet up with anyone, you need to always let someone you trust know your plans and whereabouts.

There is a great need to educate all young people on the importance of being aware of your surroundings and the tricks individuals try to play on their victims to get them to comply with their requests. The most important details can be found in the facts and this is an especially important fact. Although we teach our children to be on alert for "stranger danger," the danger may not come only from strangers. According to a 2003 National Institute of Justice report, three out of four adolescents who have been sexually assaulted were victimized by someone they knew well.

Typically, this person may try to groom you. It may start off with small gestures of kindness. It may lead to requests, making you believe what's happening isn't actually abuse. The predator tries to insight fear so the victim doesn't tell anyone.

When you feel confused or uncomfortable about what a person is teaching or offering you, be proactive and talk to a trusted adult. Just because you like someone, or they seem to demonstrate that they like you, doesn't automatically give them access to your body. Always be straightforward with people who ask to touch you inappropriately. Respond by clearly saying, "No."

Beware of Groomers!

Groomers are individuals who are skilled in knowing how to connect well to young people. They try to build trust, give gifts over time and make their victims keep secrets. They have many tricks up their sleeves and are known for testing boundaries by doing inappropriate things but making light of them. They try to intimidate or embarrass the victim based on the information they have on them and try to help the victim break rules that will lead to a vulnerable state such as drugs and alcohol.

They try to keep the lines of communication open between their victims, but everything is a secret. They prey on young people they feel won't tell them "no" because they think they lack the knowledge to recognize manipulation tactics. They work on their victims until they are able to get alone time with them. A parent, guardian, family member or good friend should always know your whereabouts.

Back to Sex!

If your peers taught you everything you need to know about sex, it's safe to say that most likely you've been misinformed. Information is exchanged and picked up from social media, culture and peers. Rarely is the information checked for validity by young minds. At your age, your perception is your reality and that's enormously powerful.

I searched through the Webster Dictionary to find three particularly important definitions for this topic: sexual intercourse, safe sex and condoms.

- Sexual intercourse is heterosexual intercourse involving penetration of the vagina by the penis.
- Safe sex is sexual activity and especially sexual intercourse in which various measures (such as the use of latex condoms or the practice of monogamy) are taken to avoid disease (such as AIDS) transmitted by sexual contact.
- Condoms are rubbers worn over the penis and a form of prevention for both pregnancy and venereal disease.

Let me enlighten you about a few things. Sex is an intimate act done by two consenting adults who should love one another and understand the consequences and implications of the act. Sex is not for kids and should not be entered into lightly. Before engaging in sexual intercourse with an individual, you should know them well and take a trip to the clinic to ensure both parties don't have a sexually transmitted disease (STD) which can cause a great unease in the days ahead.

Condoms are a good option to help keep from getting pregnant or contact a STD, but there's no guarantee that the condom won't break. Not only do condoms have to be used properly and consistently, one slip-up and your life can be altered forever. A condom must be used before any vaginal contact, even after oral sex acts. Correct removal and disposal are also important, as well as immediate replacement should a condom break.

There are other diseases you can get even if a condom is used that only require skin-to-skin contact, such as oral and genital herpes, pubic lice (crabs), HPV and syphilis, all of which are life altering.

While we are here, let's address the common misconceptions concerning sex:

- You can tell who has an STD just by looking at them.
- You can have sex and not get pregnant if you're standing up.
- "Pulling Out" is a form of birth control.
- You can't get an STD from oral sex.
- HIV can be spread through saliva or sweat.

If you take this information and put it to use, you will be in for a rude awakening, because this information is absolutely, positively *false.*

Your body is sacred, and you are a treasure that will be unveiled in due time if you choose. There is no rush to have sex, and you don't have to accept the invitation if someone is pressuring you to do it. Sex belongs within a relationship between two committed individuals.

I value waiting for marriage to have sex. Not having sex does not mean you're lacking and it won't make you any more popular for the right reason if you do. Self-esteem plays a great role in your day-to-day decisions. Take your adolescent years and become complete by working on *you* and your future goals and aspirations.

THE TEACHER

Dear Destiny,

I would like to believe that some of the most amazing people on earth are teachers. The way a teacher carries so much love for another human being and makes a commitment to cultivating the minds of a generation is selfless work. You commit yourself to pulling out the greatness in another. Every individual has to cross paths with a teacher in order to learn. I believe we all have a teacher within us.

Teachers have a different level of responsibility than most other professions. They have one job and that's to teach; but every teacher I know far exceeds those expectations. It's nearly impossible to just teach when you have minds in front of you that can be molded to become the next president, or turn a third-world country into a first-world country. Imagine the teachers who taught Prime Minister Lee Kuan Yew (LKY) of Singapore. I have to wonder what amazing teacher(s) crossed his path and what jewels of wisdom could have assisted in his endeavor to turn a country around. I also wonder the type of student he was? No matter the behavior or intellect, greatness was his final destination.

My amazing teachers taught me how to teach to a student's potential, therefore giving me a level of patience from heaven.

Hearing a student give up and coaching them, reminding them that there is no quit in them. You could have a future endocrinologist in front of you that discovers a new treatment. Your words could make the difference if the road gets tough when she pursues her studies. She will replay your positive words in her head hearing them as her own: "I can do all things."

Many teachers go far and beyond teaching. They play a role of mentor, counselor, friend, parent or nurturer, role model, and can sometimes feel like an enemy when they push you beyond your comfort zone. A great teacher controls the climate of the classroom and creates a place of safety for the students. Safety will allow a student to come alive. They will participate, assist, and even be okay with not having the right answer, but are more willing to weigh in on a conversation. Teaching students that their input matters and strengthening them to speak is so empowering for both the teacher and the student. Though some may be shy, when they speak, they often speak for others who often remain silent, and in turn educates us all.

Thank you for allowing me to be your teacher. I can only tell you "my truth," so you will have to travel your own path and make your own decisions. Always know there are consequences to your actions – both good and bad. Adolescent years are full of ups and downs, triumphs, victories, promotion, bonuses, inheritances, and muscle-building experiences. As the seasons change, so do we. Even when you don't feel it, know that life gets better; you just have to "keep on living" like the old folks say. I want you to feel safe in this world and never uncovered because the Lord protects you. You have my prayers and you've been given a great level of strength. Trust the process!

I look forward to the day that we can talk about everything and you feel comfortable telling me your truths. You're the daughter I prayed for – a safe haven, somewhere for me to lay my knowledge down and know it will live on. I love you.

– Mom

" —

WITHOUT TEACHERS,
LIFE
WOULD HAVE
NO CLASS

— "

AFFIRMATIONS OF A TEENAGE GIRL

In life, you will come to find that there are so many days that are filled with love, laughter and the smell of fresh lilies from the garden. But there will also be days that are less so. Whatever day you find yourself experiencing, repeat the selected affirmations you choose below daily to help gravitate you to an amazing place of peace within while moving toward a great outcome.

The mirror loves me.
I practice great habits.
I keep my temple clean.
I see the good in others.
I have a positive attitude.
I have a healthy lifestyle.
I am my brother's keeper.
I stand up for what's right.
I do not repay evil for evil.
I have a vision for my life.
I excel in every subject area.
I have a perfect credit score.
I have a prosperous business.
I complete the projects I start.
I have positive body language.
I am the solution to the problem.

I choose my relationships wisely.

I am invited to sit amongst the best.

I am fearfully and wonderfully made.

I practice self-discipline and etiquette.

I am quick to listen and slow to speak.

My thoughts are generated from a place of love.

I am careful with whom I associate.

I am aware of my surroundings and the beauty of this earth.

I dismiss myself from situations that will have a negative outcome.

I always make the best decisions that will result in positive outcomes.

I meditate and search for peace within; I am determined and motivated to persevere.

I have a vast imagination and I write down the creative thoughts that enter my mind.

I make an added effort to be quiet and gain wisdom from those who give of their time to lend it.

I make great decisions for my life that in turn have a positive impact on my future.

I don't allow people or situations to control my emotions – I choose my emotions.

I have the solution to someone's problem – I am a problem solver.

I respect my teachers. They pour out the knowledge that I need.

I self-access and change to become the best version of me.

I teach others through my actions and I'm also teachable.

I am not jealous, but rather happy for my peers' success.

I respect cultures and customs from around the world.

I believe there is power and freedom in forgiveness.

My non-negotiables dictate areas from which I will flee.

I complete the assignment as soon as it is given.
I will be proactive rather than reactive.
I will help to make this world a better place.
I treat others the way I want to be treated.
There is no obstacle I cannot overcome.
I respect myself and I'm well respected.
No one can be "me" better than me.
I take responsibility for my actions.
I light up the room when I enter.
I use proper etiquette every day.
I will engage in learning daily.
I am beautiful inside and out.
I love myself and I am loved.
I speak well, I listen well.
I am not a procrastinator.
I am loving and lovable.
I will seize opportunity.
I am always improving.
I have non-negotiables.
I am the competition.
I choose to be happy.
I am a high achiever.
I am uniquely made.
I am a team player.
I am a great friend.
I am a peacemaker.
I am goal-oriented.
I am a self-starter.
I am encouraged.

I am courageous.
I am supportive.
I give to charity.
I am intelligent.
I am graceful.
I am beautiful.
I seek wisdom.
I am a thinker.
I am fearless.
I am talented.
I am wealthy.
I am healthy.
I am enough.
I have favor.
I am honest.
I am unique.
I am healed.
I am strong.
I am a doer.
I love me.
I am wise.
I am safe.
I am free.
I am *me*.

BIBLIOGRAPHY

Berry, Jennifer. "Endorphins: Effects and How to Boost Them." *Medical News Today.*

MediLexicon International, 6 Feb. 2018. Web. Accessed 19 May 2020.

Dolan, Eric W. "Study Reveals Just How Quickly We Form a First Impression." *PsyPost,* 31 Oct. 2017. Web. Accessed 19 May 2020.

Message Bible. Christian Book Distributors, 1993. Web. Accessed 19 May 2020.

"About: Lee Kuan Yew." *DBPedia,* dbpedia.org/resource/Lee_Kuan_Yew.

"Wisdom." *Merriam-Webster.com Dictionary,* Merriam-Webster. Accessed 21 May 2020.

"Sexual Intercourse." *Merriam-Webster.com Dictionary,* Merriam-Webster. Web. Accessed 4 Dec. 2019.

"Safe sex." *Merriam-Webster.com Dictionary,* Merriam-Webster. Web. Accessed 21 May. 2020.

"Condom." *Merriam-Webster.com Dictionary,* Merriam-Webster. Web. Accessed 21 May. 2020.

"Attitude." *Oxford Learners Dictionary.* Web. Accessed 19 May 2020.

O'Shea, Bev. "Credit Score Ranges: How Do You Compare?" *NerdWallet,* 19 Dec. 2019. Web. Accessed 19 May 2020.

"Malala Leads World Figures in TIME Person of the Year Poll." *Time,* Time, 30 Nov. 2015.

Whitelocks, Sadie. "Relationship Expert Reveals Why Women Are Always Attracted to 'Versions of Their Fathers'." *Daily Mail Online*, Associated Newspapers, 27 May 2016.

"Education." *Wikipedia*, Wikimedia Foundation, 21 May 2020, en.wikipedia.org/wiki/Education.

Atchison, Doug. *Akeelah and the Bee. Akeelah and the Bee*, 2006.

* 9 7 8 1 7 3 4 3 9 6 5 9 1 *